ASPEN PUBLISHER

Friedman's
—— Practice Series

Administrative Law

Edited by

Professor Joel Wm. Friedman

Tulane University Law School
Jack M. Gordon Professor of Procedural Law & Jurisdiction

Wolters Kluwer
Law & Business

AUSTIN   BOSTON   CHICAGO   NEW YORK   THE NETHERLANDS

To contact Customer Care, e-mail customer.care@aspenpublishers.com, call 1-800-234-1660, fax 1-800-901-9075, or mail correspondence to:

Aspen Publishers
Attn: Order Department
PO Box 990
Frederick, MD 21705

Printed in the United States of America.

1 2 3 4 5 6 7 8 9 0

ISBN 978-0-7355-9797-6

About Wolters Kluwer Law & Business

Wolters Kluwer Law & Business is a leading provider of research information and workflow solutions in key specialty areas. The strengths of the individual brands of Aspen Publishers, CCH, Kluwer Law International and Loislaw are aligned within Wolters Kluwer Law & Business to provide comprehensive, in-depth solutions and expert-authored content for the legal, professional and education markets.

CCH was founded in 1913 and has served more than four generations of business professionals and their clients. The CCH products in the Wolters Kluwer Law & Business group are highly regarded electronic and print resources for legal, securities, antitrust and trade regulation, government contracting, banking, pension, payroll, employment and labor, and healthcare reimbursement and compliance professionals.

Aspen Publishers is a leading information provider for attorneys, business professionals and law students. Written by preeminent authorities, Aspen products offer analytical and practical information in a range of specialty practice areas from securities law and intellectual property to mergers and acquisitions and pension/benefits. Aspen's trusted legal education resources provide professors and students with high-quality, up-to-date and effective resources for successful instruction and study in all areas of the law.

Kluwer Law International supplies the global business community with comprehensive English-language international legal information. Legal practitioners, corporate counsel and business executives around the world rely on the Kluwer Law International journals, loose-leafs, books and electronic products for authoritative information in many areas of international legal practice.

Loislaw is a premier provider of digitized legal content to small law firm practitioners of various specializations. Loislaw provides attorneys with the ability to quickly and efficiently find the necessary legal information they need, when and where they need it, by facilitating access to primary law as well as state-specific law, records, forms and treatises.

Wolters Kluwer Law & Business, a unit of Wolters Kluwer, is headquartered in New York and Riverwoods, Illinois. Wolters Kluwer is a leading multinational publisher and information services company.

CHECK OUT THESE OTHER GREAT TITLES

Friedman's Practice Series

Outlining Is Important But PRACTICE MAKES PERFECT!

All Content Written By *Top Professors* • 100 Multiple Choice Questions • Comprehensive *Professor* Answers and Analysis for Multiple Choice Questions • *Real Law School* Essay Exams • Comprehensive *Professor* Answers for Essay Exams

Available titles in this series include:

Friedman's Administrative Law

Friedman's Civil Procedure

Friedman's Constitutional Law

Friedman's Contracts

Friedman's Criminal Law

Friedman's Criminal Procedure

Friedman's Property

Friedman's Torts

Friedman's Wills, Trusts, and Estates

ASK FOR THEM AT YOUR LOCAL BOOKSTORE
IF UNAVAILABLE, PURCHASE ONLINE AT *http://lawschool.aspenpublishers.com*

ABOUT THE EDITOR

Joel Wm. Friedman
Tulane Law School
Jack M. Gordon Professor of Procedural Law & Jurisdiction,
   Director of Technology
BS, 1972, Cornell University; JD, 1975, Yale University

Professor Joel Wm. Friedman, the Jack M. Gordon Professor of Procedural Law & Jurisdiction at Tulane Law School, is the lead author of two highly regarded casebooks — "The Law of Civil Procedure: Cases and Materials" (published by Thomson/West) and "The Law of Employment Discrimination" (published by Foundation Press). His many law review articles have been published in, among others, the Cornell, Texas, Iowa, Tulane, Vanderbilt, and Washington & Lee Law Reviews.

Professor Friedman is an expert in computer-assisted legal instruction who has lectured throughout the country on how law schools can integrate developing technologies into legal education. He is a past recipient of the Felix Frankfurter Teaching Award and the Sumpter Marks Award for Scholarly Achievement.

TABLE OF CONTENTS

Essay Examination Questions

Essay Examination Answers

Multiple Choice

ADMINISTRATIVE LAW
ESSAY EXAMINATION
QUESTIONS

ADMINISTRATIVE LAW ESSAY EXAM #1

QUESTION #1

One year ago, after a spate of news stories about athletes dying because of unsafe drugs they took to build muscle mass, Congress enacted "the Safe Exercise Drug Act" (SEDA). The statute reads as follows:

§1: *Findings:*

Congress hereby finds the following:

1. Drugs designed to improve athletic performance have been beneficial to both professional athletes and average Americans seeking to improve their physical fitness. Companies that produce such drugs should be allowed to continue their work with only the minimum regulation necessary to ensure public health and safety.

2. Exercise drugs, if mislabeled or unsafe, threaten public health and safety.

§2: *Regulatory Authority*

a. The Department of Agriculture is hereby authorized to promulgate regulations pertaining to the proper use and safety of exercise drugs.

b. In promulgating regulations, the agency shall take into account the particular drug's toxicity and the economic burdens of compliance.

§3: *Penalties*

Any person in violation of this law or any regulation promulgated thereunder shall be guilty of manufacturing illegal drugs, and shall be subject to the relevant criminal law penalties.

The rule ultimately promulgated by the Department reads as follows:

Reg A: No exercise drug may include stylene or monohydrene.

Your law office represents GB, Inc., a small manufacturer of "Get Big," a muscle-building powder whose main ingredient is stylene. One day, GB's general counsel calls you and explains that she's very concerned about the above regulation.

She first describes the rulemaking process: "The process was a mess. I called the agency and asked for the hearing date, and they told me there wasn't going to be any hearing. Can you believe that? They told us to put whatever we had to say in writing and mail it to them. Then a friend who lives in Washington sent me a *Washington Daily Tattler* article entitled 'Big Boys Bare Muscle on Exercise Drug Rules.' The article said that 'OMB officials were funneling technical information to the agency about possible carcinogenic effects of several exercise drugs. *Tattler* sources indicate that this technical information was provided to OMB by manufacturers of those drugs.' The article also said that, 'in addition, lobbyists hired by makers of the exercise drug bio-hydrate had cornered the head of the Department at a dinner party and tried to convince him not to ban bio-hydrate, but instead to come up with a rule "everyone could live with."' That's not fair, is it?"

She continued: "The final rule stinks. First, I don't know where the agency gets off banning any drugs; the statute doesn't authorize them to do that. Here's all the agency said about that in its announcement of the final rule:

> The agency believes that it has the authority to ban particular substances from appearing in exercise drugs. Congress acted in response to the death of athletes who took drugs that had unsafe substances. Moreover, it found that unsafe drugs threaten the public health and safety. The agency believes that these facts indicate Congress's intent to give the agency all the authority it needed to ensure the safety of these drugs, including banning certain substances within them.

"Moreover, its analysis is screwy. It explained the rule by saying that stylene and monohydrene were suspected carcinogens and that banning them would not hurt the industry much because it's so profitable. There are two problems with that. First, they used a straight-line depreciation method to figure out the industry's cost structure. It just makes more sense to use accelerated depreciation in this industry, since companies like ours are always buying newer pharmaceutical production equipment. Using the accelerated method, the industry isn't all that profitable. Here's what the agency said about this in their announcement of the rule: 'The agency has decided that straight-line depreciation is appropriate, as this is the most commonly accepted method of depreciation in U.S. industry today.' Well that's true — but *our* industry is different!

"Second, stylene may in general be a carcinogen, but not as used in our product. You see, we make a unique product: stylene mixed with seaweed. The seaweed absorbs the potential carcinogens in the stylene. In fact, we do this exactly because serious body builders take large quantities of our product, and we wanted to ensure that they wouldn't get cancer. No other company uses seaweed to detoxify its product. Again, the agency didn't really consider this: here is all they said: 'The agency has considered the arguments that addition of other materials to a drug containing stylene may mitigate stylene's carcinogenic effects. However, such claims are unproven, and, until that claim is proven, the agency believes that erring on the side of caution is the best policy.' Phooey! OK, it's true we didn't give them clinical proof. But nobody's ever gotten cancer from our product, so far as we know."

She concludes: "We need to stop this regulation, and stop it now. As soon as it's effective, we will be in violation of the law and subject to penalties as drug traffickers!"

Answer the following questions:

1. Can GB sue the agency in federal court and attack the general validity of the regulation? Can it sue now?
2. What claims, about either the agency's procedure or the substance of its rule, arise from the above facts? Evaluate the chances of success on each of these claims.

Note: Excerpts from *Thompson's Treatise on Statutory Interpretation*, a standard reference work for statutory interpretation issues, are reprinted below. You may choose to use that source if you wish, but you don't have to.

§4.10: *Plain Meaning:* A statute should be accorded its plain meaning, no more and no less. A statute's words should not be twisted, compressed, or stretched, even in the service of a desirable policy objective.

§8.7: *Health and Safety Regulation:* Statutes protecting the health and safety of the public should be given a generous reading, to accomplish their beneficent goal.

QUESTION #2

Ned is a mid-level manager for the Department of Human Services of the State of Utopia. Ned has worked at the department for five years. It is department policy to employ mid-level managers on one-year contracts, but in the last 20 years, only 2 out of 300 mid-level managers have left because the department decided not to renew their contracts. (Assume that standard civil-service job security rules do not apply.) The department's employment manual reads as follows:

> Mid-Level Managers: The Department believes in the stability of its mid-level management team. Thus, any mid-level manager who is happy and productive and an asset to the Department can expect to remain employed with the Department.

The manual also reads as follows:

> Dismissals: Any dismissal for any reason is final unless the Department itself decides to reconsider the case. In case of a dismissal, the employee shall have the right to submit written comments and materials tending to show why he or she should not be dismissed but has no right to an oral hearing until after an adverse dismissal decision. After that decision, the dismissal is effective; should the oral hearing lead to the employee's rehiring, he or she will NOT be paid the lost salary. Oral hearings, if requested, shall be held within six months of any firing decision.

One day, as his fifth one-year contract was nearing its end, Ned was summoned to his supervisor's office. He thought this meeting would be for the purpose of signing his next contract, but instead the supervisor told him that "he just wasn't working out" and that his current contract would not be renewed.

Ned files suit against the department.

Analyze his procedural due process argument. You may assume that Ned has available five years of written performance reviews.

ADMINISTRATIVE LAW ESSAY EXAM #2

QUESTION #1

One day your boss calls you into his office. He hands you the following materials: a federal statute called the "Climate Protection Act" ("Act" or "CPA"), a *Federal Register* item from the previous day, and an excerpt from a treatise on statutory interpretation. He asks you to read them in his office while he obsessively plays with a rubber band.

THE CLIMATE PROTECTION ACT

§1: *Findings*
The Congress hereby finds the following:
  (a) that human-induced climate change poses a major threat to all humans, to human civilization, and to the world's and the nation's wealth and prosperity;
  (b) as the world's largest economy, America must set an example for other nations in combating this risk; and
  (c) all Americans have a right to a climate that is stable and conducive to the continuation of civilization, consistent with economic growth and the perpetuation of the current standard of living enjoyed by the American people.

§2: *Regulatory Authority*
  (a) The Environmental Protection Agency (EPA or Agency) shall promulgate regulations to ensure, to the extent feasible considering technological feasibility, economic prosperity, and the state of climatological knowledge, that the global climate is not subject to unreasonable risk of serious deterioration or instability.
  (b) Such regulations shall be promulgated after fair hearing.
  (c) After promulgated, such regulations shall be transmitted to the Senate Committee on the Environment and the House Special Committee on Climate Change for review. Such regulations shall not take effect until 60 days after such transmission.

One year after enactment of the statute, the following notice appeared in the *Federal Register*:

NOTICE OF FINAL RULE
(Statutory Authority: Climate Protection Act)

The EPA hereby announces Reg CPA-2010-03, promulgated under the Agency's regulatory authority pursuant to the CPA.

Reg. 2010-03: New homes in the United States shall not be constructed with a fireplace.

A. *Background*

The CPA requires the Agency to promulgate regulations "to ensure, to the extent feasible considering technological feasibility, economic prosperity, and the state of climatological knowledge, that the global climate is not subject to unreasonable risk of serious deterioration or instability." CPA §2(a). Immediately upon enactment of the CPA, the agency commenced studying how design of a whole panoply of items could be improved so as to reduce those items' effect on climate change.

The Agency announced a proposed regulation on home design eight months ago. *See* 73 *Fed. Reg.* 2569 ([dated eight months before]) (the "proposed regulation"). The proposed regulation read as follows:

Proposed Regulation: Home heating and cooling systems shall be designed to achieve maximum effectiveness with minimum impact on the global climate.

In response to comments to the proposed regulation received during the three-month comment period, the agency today promulgates Reg. CPA-2010-03.

B. The Agency's Analysis

1. Definitional Issues

1. The Agency faced a number of questions when considering both the proposed regulation and the final regulation announced today. First, it had to ensure that the regulation conformed to the mandate handed down by Congress. In particular, it had to consider the meaning of the phrase "unreasonable risk of serious deterioration or instability" in §2(a). On one reading, this phrase might suggest regulatory authority only to ensure that the global climate is not subject to a *significant* risk of deterioration or instability, on the theory that only significant risks are "*unreasonable* risks of *serious* [climate] deterioration or instability" (italics added). A number of comments to the proposed regulation offered this interpretation.[*] Unsurprisingly, these comments were accompanied by arguments that home heating and cooling systems did not pose a significant risk of serious climate deterioration or instability, given the fact that such systems account for a very small part of what we know about the causes of global climate change.

However, on reflection during the post-comment period, the Agency concluded that the better reading of the phrase "unreasonable risk of serious deterioration or instability" referred to a risk that was "unreasonable" in terms of the balance between the climate risks and the social benefits of the particular activity being regulated. Both common use and specialized legal use of language supports this conclusion. See, *e.g.*, *Webster's New American Dictionary 459* (12th ed. 2005), defining "unreasonable" to mean, among other things, "inappropriate or excessive *in relation to countervailing factors or benefits*"; and *Black's Law Dictionary 344* (10th ed. 2001), defining "unreasonable" to mean, among other things, "that

---

[*] In response to the proposed regulation, some individuals sent interrogatories to the agency asking for technical data relevant to the proposed regulation. The requests were denied, given the lack of any legal duty to engage in such procedural formalities.

which a person of average intelligence and judgment would consider outside a broad band of appropriate conduct, *in light of the entire situation facing such a person*" (italics added in both cases).

Moreover, such an interpretation would avoid the regulatory problems that would follow from requiring that before an activity could be regulated, it would have to contribute substantially to the problem of climate change. Aside from the difficult line-drawing problems that would arise if the agency attempted to determine which activities contributed *substantially* to climate change, such an interpretation would essentially limit the agency's authority to activities with large-scale or particularly egregious effects on the climate. In the Agency's view, this result would contradict Congress's clear desire to take a strong stand against global warming, even at the cost of prohibiting traditionally enjoyed conduct that contributes only marginally to climate change. In this vein, it is appropriate to note that we still know little about how small an amount of climate change will cause serious impacts — for example, if there are "tipping points" where even small climate changes will cause serious impacts. It is also worth noting that it is the policy of the current Administration to take a strong stand against global warming, both for its own sake and also to encourage other nations to do so as well. Such cooperation also serves the government's larger purpose of encouraging global cooperation on a whole host of non–climate-related issues.

For these reasons, the Agency concludes that §2(a) clearly states the rule governing the Agency's action.

C. The Agency's Policy Choices

In light of this understanding of the statute, the Agency then proceeded to consider the appropriateness of the regulation it originally proposed. First, the Agency notes the comments many home builders offered to the proposed regulation, to the effect that further regulation of most home heating and cooling systems is simply unnecessary given that consumers' demand for economical home operation has already made such systems highly efficient. These comments convinced the agency to take a closer look at the one home heating system that is essentially as inefficient today as it was 100 years ago: fireplaces. The Agency has received no information contradicting a study it commissioned two years ago, which concluded that modern fireplaces retained their historical inefficiencies and that their very simplicity suggested that few, if any, design changes could be made to mitigate them. Such a lack of efficiency is not surprising: it is commonly understood that most residential users of fireplaces are motivated by the aesthetics and atmosphere provided by a fire, rather than by a sense that it provides an efficient heating system.

Thus, fireplaces present an "unreasonable risk of serious [climate] deterioration or instability," §2(a), despite the undisputed fact that they constitute, in an absolute sense, a trivial contribution to the problem of global climate change.

After you're finished reading, the boss addresses you again. "We represent the American Association of Home Builders. They are really steamed at this. This regulation will make older homes that already have fireplaces far more desirable than new homes. Indeed, it looks like the reg will stop the construction of homes for which the foundations have already been laid and contracts already signed — foundations and contracts that assume a house with a fireplace! They want this reg killed.

"I talked to the association's regulatory monitor about this. He told me that they were completely flabbergasted by this rule. He told me that after the proposed reg came out last fall, everyone thought that the agency was just going to impose some efficiency requirements for central air and heating systems, stuff that the association would be happy with because consumer pressure was already forcing builders in that same direction. I asked him about the agency's statements about fireplace efficiency, and he told me that he had no idea what the agency was talking about. He didn't see anything about it in the *Federal Register* announcement of the proposed reg, and he tells me that he sent an interrogatory to the agency asking for any technical studies and got back a form letter stating that the agency was under no legal duty to comply.

"We're having a conference call with the association in a few minutes. I need you to write a quick memo with all the possible attacks we can make on the statute and whether you think they might succeed. Don't worry about standing or the timing of the lawsuit; we can deal with those issues later. And don't worry about the format of the memo; just make it like an answer to a law school exam."

Create the memo that the boss requests. If you don't have time to analyze all the issues, at least identify them.

Note: You can assume that the association's interrogatories to the agency do **NOT** constitute a request for information under the Freedom of Information Act (FOIA). Do **NOT** analyze FOIA in your answer.

QUESTION #2

One day, you are working at an immigration-law clinic in Los Angeles when you meet Ben Navarro, an Argentinean citizen who does not have a valid federal work permit. Ben was fired from his engineering job at Bing Aerospace. He tells you that he was fired because he complained about working conditions that violated California law. His attorney filed a claim under the Federal Safe Workplace Act (FSWA), reprinted below. The Department of Labor administrative law judge (ALJ) who heard the claim ruled in favor of Bing because of Navarro's status as an illegal worker. Navarro now wants to appeal to a federal court.

The applicable federal law, the FSWA, reads as follows:

Section 1: *Definitions* . . .

(d) "Employee" means any person lawfully employed by an employer pursuant to federal law and state law.

Section 2: *Employee Protection*

Any employer who fires any employee as a direct result of the employee's notification to the employer of a condition that violates applicable federal or state working conditions law shall be liable for back pay and treble damages.

Section 3: *Regulations*

The Department of Labor shall promulgate regulations, after hearing, to implement this statute.

Section 4: *Adjudication of Claims*

Claims made under this statute shall be heard in the first instance by administrative law judges (ALJs) inside the Department of Labor, who shall adjudicate such claims on the record after opportunity for an agency hearing.

Several months before the ALJ's decision, the Department of Labor caused the following announcement to be printed in the *Federal Register:*

Department of Labor
Federal Safe Workplaces Act
Promulgation of Regulation 02-A

Officer in Charge of Regulation: Mary Martin

1. Regulation

Today the Department of Labor ("the Department") promulgates a regulation intended to clarify an issue that has arisen in litigation under the FSWA.

Reg 02-A: The statutory language "any person lawfully employed by an employer pursuant to federal law and state law" refers to an employment relationship that both satisfies the requirements of the employment law of the state in which the employee is employed, and federal immigration law.

2. Background and Explanation

The regulation promulgated today grows out of questions that have arisen concerning the status of workers who are not U.S. citizens and who do not hold valid work permits. Today the Department concludes that the statute, as best understood, does in fact require, in order for someone to be a protected "employee," that his or her employment not violate applicable federal immigration law.

The Department reached this conclusion for several reasons:
   1. We believe that this reading gives full effect to every word in the statute. The statute defines "employee" as a person lawfully employed "pursuant to federal law *and* state law" (FSWA, Section 1; italics added). The statute's reference to both federal law and state law suggests that the legality of the employment relationship be judged by reference to federal, as well as state, law. Dictionaries suggest that we are interpreting the word "pursuant" correctly.
   2. Commenters[*] on this proposed rule suggested that the interpretation adopted today is not necessary to give effect to all the words in a statute, since there is a body of federal labor law, for example the National Labor Relations Act, to which the statute might have been referring when it cited federal law. Nevertheless, the Department believes, especially given the attacks of September 11, that immigration status should be a factor in the administration of every federal regulatory program wherever it might even arguably apply. This is in conformance with the President's stated goal to

---

[*] Various parties requested an oral hearing as part of the rulemaking process. The Department denied these requests, since such hearings are not required by law and, in the Department's view, would not have added helpful information.

make every federal agency responsible, within its own sphere of authority, for homeland security.

3. Commenters also pointed out that immigration status has never before been thought to deny worker protection under other labor law statutes. In particular, commenters pointed to the National Labor Relations Act Amendments of 1947, which defines "employee" in exactly the same way as under the FSWA, but which has never been construed to involve immigration status in the determination whether an individual is an employee. Commenters also suggested that Congress "ratified" this prior understanding by re-enacting this definition in the FSWA, against the backdrop of the Department's consistent failure to incorporate immigration status in the determination of who is an "employee" "pursuant to federal law." The Department appreciates this argument, but respectfully suggests that such legislative "ratification" of a long-standing agency interpretation has no place in the appropriate determination by an agency of a statute's meaning, especially when, as here, Congress has explicitly delegated that interpretive task to the agency.

After being assigned Navarro's case, your preliminary research yields the following:

1. Your FOIA request yielded a document entitled "Minutes of Meeting Between Mary Martin and Department of Labor Chief Counsel," dated December 28 of last year. This document indicates that Martin and the staff counsel engaged in a broad-ranging discussion of the statute and its appropriate interpretation, including a discussion of the data dealing with the employment of illegal aliens in American businesses.
2. In your research of statutory interpretation issues, you find several aids to interpreting the statute, reprinted below.
3. Your examination of the record made before the ALJ reveals that the hearing that Navarro described was simply a paper hearing, without the opportunity for the calling of witnesses. The ALJ's order simply states that such oral testimony "is generally not required under the APA, and for that reason the [ALJ] will not allow it in this case."

EXHIBIT A

Black's Law Dictionary, 5th ed. (1979):

Pursuant: . . . " 'pursuant to' means 'in the course of carrying out: in conformance to or agreement with; according to' and, when used in a statute, is a restrictive term"

Simon's New International Dictionary, 2d ed. (1954):

Pursuant: "Agreeably, conformably, according"

Simon's Seventh New Collegiate Dictionary (1967):

Pursuant: "In carrying out; in conformance to; according to"

EXHIBIT B

Excerpts from *Thompson's Treatise on Statutory Interpretation*, 5th ed. (2000).

Note: This is a standard reference work for statutory interpretation issues.

§46.06 *Each word given effect.*

It is fundamental to sound statutory interpretation that, if possible, effect must be given to every word, clause, and sentence of a statute.

What arguments could Navarro make about either the regulation or the hearing that he received in front of the ALJ?

> ## ADMINISTRATIVE LAW ESSAY EXAM #3

> ## QUESTION #1

Hal Robinson is a veteran of the Second Gulf War and the father of Diana, a 5-year-old girl. Ever since she was born, Diana has received free medical care from the government, due to Hal's status as a veteran, under the Veterans Dependent Health Care Program ("Program"), a program administered by the Department of Veterans' Affairs ("Agency"). The statute states that dependents of veterans are eligible for medical care if they are "actually dependent" on the veteran.

In April 2010, Hal divorced Wilma, his wife of 12 years and Diana's mother. Pursuant to their agreement, Wilma obtained custody of Diana. Two months later, Hal received a letter from the Agency, stating that Diana's eligibility for the Program had terminated as of the date of the divorce. The letter is reproduced below, as Exhibit A.

Hal comes into your office, seeking help. He explains that the divorce decree explicitly deprives him of custodial status, which is standard when custody is given to the other parent. (You may assume this is a correct general principle of family law.) He also explains that while the decree does not officially provide for any visitation or child support, he and Wilma divorced amicably, and they have informal custody and child support arrangements, which are memorialized in a document drafted by the couple and signed by both, but they have never been shown to anyone else and are not part of the divorce decree. Both parents want Diana to have the benefit of the Program, and Wilma is willing to testify about the existence of their informal custody and child support arrangements. Hal wants a chance for him and Wilma to testify before the benefit is cut off.

EXHIBIT A
LETTER FROM DEPARTMENT OF VETERANS AFFAIRS
TO HAL ROBINSON

Dear Mr. Robinson:

This letter is to inform you that, as of the date of the entry of your divorce decree granting custody of your child, Diana Robinson, to her mother, Diana's eligibility for the Program is terminated, as she no longer is eligible pursuant to the statute and applicable regulations.

You may appeal this decision by submitting adequate documentation to show that in fact, Diana is "actually dependent" on you, as provided for in the statute and applicable regulations. Should you lose that appeal, you may, if you wish, request an oral hearing before an administrative law judge. You should be advised, however, that, due to a shortage of administrative law judges, oral hearings are typically held not earlier than 12 months after the request is made. You may not request an oral hearing until you have lost your first appeal.

During the pendency of these two appeals processes, and commencing as of the date of this letter, Diana may not seek free medical care under the Program.

Should Diana ultimately be determined to be eligible for the Program, any reasonable and necessary medical expenses incurred for Diana's care during the pendency of your appeal(s) may be billed to the Agency.

Sincerely,

William T. Jackson
Regional Director, Department of Veterans Affairs

EXHIBIT B
Excerpts from the Veterans' Dependent Care Health Act of 2002

Section 2: Program

Minor children who are actually dependent on their veteran parents shall be eligible for care under the Veterans' Dependent Health Care Program.

Section 3: Administration

The program shall be administered by the Department of Veterans Affairs ("Agency").

Section 4: Regulations

The Agency shall promulgate regulations to administer this program.

Section 4: Preclusion of Review

The Agency's decisions made in the course of administering this program shall not be reviewed by any federal court. No decision granting or denying benefits under this program shall be subject to judicial review of any sort.

EXHIBIT C
Department of Veterans Affairs Regulation 03-2189

Eligibility Under Veterans' Dependent Health Care Act
Eligibility under the Act is limited to children under the age of 18 who have a current, official, and legally valid custodial status with a veteran, unless compelling circumstances make such a status impracticable or not in the best interest of the dependent.

Procedures for Determining Eligibility
[The Regulation sets forth the procedures noted in the letter in Exhibit A, including the provision for reimbursement of any "reasonable and necessary" medical expenses incurred during the appeals process, if the appeal is ultimately successful.]

EXHIBIT D
EXCERPT FROM THE *FEDERAL REGISTER* OF MAY 19, 2003

. . . Today, the Agency issues regulations clarifying the Veterans' Dependent Health Care Act. . . .
   1. *Procedures*: [In this part of the statement, the Agency set forth the procedures for determining eligibility, explained above.]

2. *Eligibility Standards*: The Agency has interpreted the term "actually dependent" to require that the dependent have "a current, official, and legally valid custodial status with a veteran" in order to be eligible for the Program, unless compelling circumstances make such a status impracticable or not in the best interest of the dependent. The Agency took this step for several reasons.

First, we believe that the term "actually dependent" reveals an intent to go beyond material dependency. It is the Agency's view that the only types of long-term, stable relationships Congress wished to encourage via the Program are those that are sanctioned by law. The Agency does not deny that many veterans have informal, yet loving relationships with dependents for whom they provide material and emotional support, but such relationships are of a lesser stature than legally recognized ones. We believe that the use of the qualifier "actually" in the statutory term indicates a desire on the part of Congress to limit the Program only to these deeper relationships.

Second, interpreting the term this way accords with the President's pro-family agenda. The President has directed all agencies, within the scope of their authority, to adopt policies that strengthen families. Interpreting "actually dependent" so as to equate relationships outside of legally recognized custodial relationships with legally recognized ones denigrates legally recognized unions and conflicts with the President's agenda.

The agency added an exception to this rule, for compelling circumstances. This is a narrow exception, but the Agency thought it appropriate because the diversity of family relationships and statuses is such that, in a small set of unusual cases, the equities may be such that the dependent should remain eligible for the Program.

Finally, the Agency recognizes that in the notice-and-comment process, several commenters questioned the constitutionality of the interpretation ultimately adopted by the agency. These commenters argued that this interpretation infringed on the constitutional rights of non-custodial and non-marital fathers to government recognition of their parent-child relationships. The Agency does not believe these arguments to be well taken.

1. Think about the legal claims that Hal could make. Which, if any, could he raise with a federal court? Would a federal court have jurisdiction to hear such claims? In answering this question, do **NOT** discuss any issues relating to the timing of the lawsuit.
2. Assume that Hal wants to be the plaintiff, not Diana or Wilma. Would he have standing to raise the claims that you identified in Question 1?
3. Regardless of your answers to Questions 1 and 2, analyze the merits of the claims that you identified in Question 1. Would they be successful? Why or why not?

QUESTION #2

In resolving a particularly thorny question, an administrative decision maker engages in the following confidential conversations:

1. A discussion of the technical issues relevant to the question, with an expert that is located inside the agency but who has not otherwise participated in the decision-making process.
2. A discussion at a bar association conference with a lobbyist for the industry, who is very interested in the outcome but has not otherwise participated in the decision-making process, when the discussion centers on the lobbyist's arguments in favor of a particular outcome for the issue before the decision maker.

Discuss whether these conversations are legal if the agency is engaging in the following procedures:

1. Informal rulemaking.
2. Formal rulemaking.
3. Formal adjudication.

ADMINISTRATIVE LAW ESSAY EXAM #4

QUESTION #1

One day, Roberta Rainmaker, your boss at the law firm where you work, comes into your office with a problem. Her client, the Beef Association, is an association of cattle ranchers and beef processors. In recent decades, beef producers have used Red Dye #5 (RD5), a dye that gives beef a deep red appearance, as opposed to its natural reddish-brown appearance that, according to research, consumers associate with poor-quality beef. RD5 is produced by synthesizing it, in a sophisticated chemical process, from a combination of cow intestines and chicken livers.

Last year, Congress rewrote the nation's food color additive laws. The statute is reproduced here:

THE SAFE FOOD COLOR ADDITIVES ACT

Section 1

The Congress hereby finds that food color additives make food more attractive and thus encourage consumption, but that some food additives may be carcinogenic.

Section 2
  A. The Secretary of Agriculture shall promulgate regulations that adequately ensure that the public health is not excessively impaired by use of artificial food color additives.
  B. The Secretary shall not have the authority to promulgate regulations concerning the use of naturally occurring food color additives.
  C. In promulgating these regulations, the Secretary shall consider the following factors:
    1. Human health in general;
    2. The risks to human health presented by the use of a given food color additive; and
    3. The dietary habits of average Americans.

Roberta shows you an item from the *Federal Register* dated two weeks ago, giving notice of the Department of Agriculture's promulgation of final regulations regarding food color additives. Excerpts from that item are reproduced below. In that notice, the agency stated that it interpreted the term "naturally occurring" **NOT** to include RD5. Thus, RD5 is an artificial additive subject to the regulations that the Secretary could promulgate.

Turning to the substance of the regulation, Roberta shows you a copy of the relevant regulation. It reads as follows:

Reg A: Artificial food color additives shall not be used in beef or beef by-products, unless such color additives are shown to pose a cancer risk of less than 0.01 percent over a lifetime, assuming the beef consumption of the average American in 2000.

Roberta also shows you an article appearing in the *Washington Daily Tattler* edition from two weeks ago, entitled "White House Sees Red Over Food Color Additives." The gist of the article was that the regulations were the subject of an internal struggle within the White House, with the Agriculture Department promulgating the regulations despite opposition from the White House Office of Management and Budget (OMB). According to the article, the OMB protested that the agency had not cleared the regulations pursuant to the Executive Order dealing with OMB review of proposed agency regulations. The article also quoted the Agriculture Department official who drafted the regulations, who defended them by describing them as "the product of many nights and holidays [he] spent slaving away in internal meetings with agency specialists." Roberta scoffs when she reads you that quote, sneering that the agency "was too afraid to hold an oral hearing" and that with her courtroom skills, she "could have nailed those idiots to the wall" on cross-examination and succeeded in having the regulations watered down.

Roberta then continues by discussing how the rulemaking process went. "First, the agency never gave us their toxicological assumptions and analysis explaining how the 0.01 percent cancer risk was deemed excessive. Second, they refused to answer interrogatories that we sent them about the use of 2000 consumption figures. I mean, I know interrogatories are not mentioned in the APA, but we're talking about basic issues of human health and the survival of an entire industry! Anyway, the whole idea of using 2000 numbers is nuts. Everybody knows that beef consumption is down from 2000, so using 2000 numbers artificially inflates the amount of RD5 that people actually consume. Third, they just misread the statute. What a bunch of fools — they don't even know what 'natural' means!"

Roberta continued: "So we need to act fast. The regs take effect in exactly three weeks. Every day that goes by, the Association gets inquiries about the regulations. Cattle farmers are wondering how many head of cattle they should raise for next year, given what will happen to demand for beef if we don't get these regs struck down. Everyone is afraid that there will end up being a glut of beef on the marketplace that we won't be able to sell because consumers won't have a chance to get accustomed to how it really looks. We have a conference call with the client in a little less than an hour, so write your thoughts down on paper. The basic idea is, we need to get this regulation struck down!"

In addition to the statute and excerpts from the *Federal Register* notice below, there is an excerpt from *Thompson's Treatise on Statutory Interpretation*, a standard reference tool for statutory interpretation issues. If it is relevant to your answer, you may assume that the association's by-laws state that it exists "in order to promote the interests of America's cattle ranchers."

FEDERAL REGISTER [DATED TWO WEEKS AGO]

Today, the Agriculture Department announces new standards for food color additives . . .

I. *Scope of the Regulation*

. . . The agency believes that the statute is best understood as exempting from regulation only those food additives that exist in their complete form in nature, or are easily extracted, in their final form, from natural sources. By contrast, "naturally occurring" should not be read to include additives that are produced only through the intermediation of a chemical process. "Naturally occurring," the relevant statutory term, suggests material that is present in nature. See, *e.g., Webster's Seventh Collegiate New Dictionary* (defining "natural" in part as "occurring in conformity with the ordinary course of nature" and "existing in or produced by nature"). The normal reading of that term thus contrasts with "not naturally occurring"; that is, additives that are created from constituent elements in the laboratory. The following is a list of food color additives whose regulation was considered by the agency, and an explanation of whether the statute gives the agency authority to regulate that particular additive . . .

> C. RD5: The constituent elements of RD5 exist in cow and chicken organs, but combine to produce RD5 only after a chemical process; thus RD5 is subject to regulation under the statute. . . .

II. *The Agency's Regulatory Choices*

A.   In General

EPA received many comments concerning the agency's decisions about which food color additives to ban, and for what uses. The agency is aware that some of the regulatory thresholds it uses (for example, the 0.01 percent extra cancer risk for additives to beef) are quite low, so low as to be insignificant under many theories of regulation. However, it is the agency's position that such low thresholds are appropriate when limiting use of additives in foods that are relatively less important to the overall health of the American people. Again using the example of beef, it is the agency's position that a lower exposure level is appropriate, since most Americans already consume adequate amounts of protein, the main benefit of beef consumption. Thus, any reduced consumption of beef that flows from its less attractive appearance will generally not be harmful to Americans' overall health. Indeed, to the extent that the low exposure level for beef leads to less use of color additives and beef and thus diverts consumer choices toward healthier foods, the effect of the low exposure level may even be more positive than might otherwise be thought. . . .

B.   Consumption Assumptions

Consumption assumptions were also the subject of many comments. Perhaps predictably, groups representing food interests whose consumption is rising argued for using older consumption data, while groups representing food interests whose consumption is declining argued that such older data unfairly inflated the perceived risk from allowing additives in those foods. Ultimately, the agency decided that an objective baseline figure would be impossible to find, and thus decided to use data from the last comprehensive government survey of American dietary habits, which was in 2000. Not only is this data the most comprehensive available, but since the general consensus is that the American diet has grown healthier in the last several years, use of 2000 data, if it is inaccurate, probably errs by inflating the consumption of unhealthy foods. The effect of this inflation is to impose more severe limitations on the use of additives in less healthy foods, and thus will probably divert consumption toward healthier foods, consistent with the overall statutory goal.

EXCERPT FROM *THOMPSON'S TREATISE ON STATUTORY INTERPRETATION*

Interpretive Canon 4.5: *Plain Meaning.* Usually, statutes must be read to have the plain meaning that their words convey.

Can the association sue? When? What procedural claims could it make? What substantive claims? What would the likely outcomes be?

QUESTION #2

As part of its reporting on cheating in colleges, *NewsTime*, a weekly newsmagazine, files an FOIA request with the Department of the Army, requesting all records relating to academic dishonesty investigations at the U.S. Military Academy at West Point over the last 10 years. The Department of the Army resists disclosure, and *NewsTime* sues. In addition, Sam Howell, who graduated from West Point three years ago and was falsely accused of cheating while a student there, brings his own suit, seeking to enjoin disclosure of his records. The two cases are consolidated before the same court.

You are the clerk to the judge hearing the case. What are the major principles of FOIA governing *NewsTime*'s and Howell's claims?

> ## ADMINISTRATIVE LAW ESSAY EXAM #5

> ## QUESTION #1

Congress, alarmed by several incidents in which individuals attempting to purchase items over the Internet were the victims of identity theft when their credit card information was hacked into, enacts the "Internet Commerce Promotion and Protection Act" (ICPPA). The statute reads as follows:

§1: *Findings:* The Congress hereby finds that commerce on the Internet presents a new opportunity for economic growth, but that this growth can be realized only if potential customers can reasonably believe that Internet transactions are technologically safe and secure. The Congress also finds that Americans have the right to Internet transactions that are as secure as face-to-face transactions. Congress also finds that the rapidly changing nature of the Internet requires judges evaluating these matters be technically expert.

§2: *Definitions:*

   A.   "Internet Business" means any person, corporation, or other entity that customarily offers goods or services for sale on the Internet.

§3: *Safety of Internet Transactions:* Internet Businesses shall, to the extent feasible, ensure the maximum safety of Internet transactions.

§4: *Implementation Authority:* There is hereby created the Office of Internet Commerce (the "agency"), within the Department of Commerce and whose head is under the supervision of the Secretary of Commerce. The department is authorized and directed to promulgate regulations to implement the policy reflected in this statute.

§5: *Legislative Oversight:* Congress may overturn any regulation promulgated pursuant to §4 of this statute, upon a majority vote of both houses of Congress.

§6: *Appointment and Removal:* The President shall appoint the head of the agency. He may be removed for good cause, either by the President or the Congress, but only for good cause.

§7: *Fines:* Any Internet Business violating this statute or any valid regulation promulgated pursuant to §4 shall be liable for a fine of at least $5,000 per violation.

§8: *Adjudication of Fines:* Persons injured by the violation of this law or any regulation promulgated thereunder may bring a suit in a court, to be housed in the agency and staffed by an Administrative Law Judge (ALJ) within the FTC. Such ALJs shall serve for periods of five years before returning to regular employee status in the agency, and shall always be subject to dismissal under applicable Civil Service rules. The ALJ shall have the jurisdiction to hear any counter-claims growing out of the facts giving rise to the plaintiff's original claim. The ALJ shall have the power to enforce its own orders.

Appeals from any such ALJ decision may be made to the "Internet Commerce Court," which shall be comprised of rotating panels of three federal judges.

The Internet Commerce Court shall reverse any factual findings or legal conclusions found to be clearly erroneous. The decisions of this court shall be final and not subject to further review.

What constitutional issues are raised by the statute?

QUESTION #2

The federal Clean Water Act (the "statute") authorizes EPA personnel above the rank of "deputy assistant regional coordinator" to issue what are called "temporary discharge permits" ("temporary permits"). Basically, these are permits designed to allow a polluter to increase its discharges temporarily for short periods of time — for example, when a piece of pollution equipment is being repaired. The statute states that temporary permits apply only to the particular time period and location for which they are requested. The statute also makes clear that they can be revoked at any time and warns that third parties should not rely on any analysis in such permits. Such permits are not publicly disclosed, nor does the agency have to engage in any particular process before a qualified official issues one. Finally, the statute states that any permit may be revoked at any time. Last year, there were 875 EPA personnel, located in 50 regional offices around the country, authorized to issue temporary permits, and they issued 32,000 such permits.

One such permit interprets the Clean Water Act in a way that the requester, Ackerman Plastics, disagrees with. Ackerman sues, alleging that the agency misread the statute.

Explain the level of deference that a court would likely give that interpretation, and how a court would likely arrive at that conclusion. Explain what that level of deference entails and how it differs from other competing deference levels.

Administrative Law
Essay Examination
ANSWERS

ADMINISTRATIVE LAW ESSAY EXAM #1

QUESTION #1

I. Can GB Sue?

A. Jurisdiction: Jurisdiction in a federal court would present no problem. The APA itself does not confer jurisdiction to sue an agency. Neither does SEDA. However, GB could invoke a court's general federal question jurisdiction, 28 U.S.C. §1331, which would suffice.

B. Reviewability: The first issue here is reviewability. There is a presumption that agency action is reviewable [*e.g., Block v. Community Nutrition Institute*, 467 U.S. 340 (1984), (noting this presumption)]. The exceptions — for preclusion by statute and for action committed to agency discretion by law — do not apply here. First, the statute says nothing about precluding judicial review. Second, the standard for action committed to agency discretion by law — whether the statute is written so broadly that there is "no law to apply" — is clearly not met here; *i.e.*, the statute clearly provides a sufficient legal standard that a court could apply. Compare with *Citizens to Preserve Overton Park v. Volpe*, 401 U.S. 402 (1971), finding the statute there similarly definite. Thus, this action is reviewable.

C. Standing: The next question is whether GB has standing. Standing has both a constitutional and a prudential component.

1. Constitutional Standing: Article III requires that a plaintiff (1) be injured, (2) that the injury be caused by the defendant, and (3) that the injury be redressable by a court. The injury must be concrete and be either actual or imminent [*Lujan v. Defenders of Wildlife*, 504 U.S. 555 (1992)]. Here, GB is clearly injured by the agency's action, which will affect its business operations and profits. The injury is at least imminent, given the promulgation of the regulation. It is also caused by the agency, and an injunction against the regulation would redress its injury.

2. Prudential Standing: Section 702 of the APA has been interpreted to impose a prudential standing bar that the plaintiff must be "arguably within the zone of interests sought to be protected by the statute" [*Assn of Data Processing Serv. Organizations v. Camp*, 397 U.S. 150 (1970)]. This is a very lenient test to meet, and GB would surely meet it. The statute itself notes the benefits of exercise drugs and provides at least some protection for their continued manufacture. Thus, GB would satisfy the zone of interests test.

Thus, GB satisfies both constitutional and prudential requirements for standing.

D. Timing of Judicial Review: Timing in this context implicates two issues: finality and ripeness.

1. Finality: APA Section 704 requires that an agency action be final before it is subject to judicial review. To be final, (1) agency action must mark the consummation of the agency's decision-making process, and (2) the action must be one by which rights or obligations have been determined, or from which legal consequences will follow [*Bennett v. Spear*, 520 U.S. 154 (1997)]. Here, promulgation of a regulation would satisfy these requirements: it clearly marks the culmination of the agency's rulemaking process, and the ensuing rule creates legal obligations for GB. Thus, the action is final.

2. The final question is whether GB's lawsuit would be ripe.   The general rule is that pre-enforcement review of an agency regulation is allowed so long as the issue is appropriate for judicial resolution in the absence of further factual developments, and the private party would face hardship if it had to wait for the agency to commence an enforcement action before it could sue. Here, the purely legal issues surrounding the rule are clearly amenable to judicial resolution at this early phase. Moreover, the harm that GB would face — criminal penalties for breaking drug laws — would likely qualify as sufficient hardship. Thus, GB's challenge would be ripe.

II. Claims on the Merits

A. Procedural Claims

1. Formal v. Informal Rulemaking: This is clearly a case where only informal rulemaking is required. The statute does not even come close to the "magic words" ("on the record after opportunity for agency hearing) required by *Florida East Coast RR v. United States*, 410 U.S. 224 (1973). Thus, only informal rulemaking, which does not require an oral hearing, is called for.

2. OMB Funneling of Information: This raises an issue of the conduct required by the executive orders overseeing the regulatory process and any remedies for violations of those orders. The orders in effect since the early 1990s have generally restricted OMB's ability to funnel information to an agency through back channels of this sort, given how that sort of funneling frustrates the public rulemaking process by essentially creating a shadow process shielded from public view. In general, OMB is allowed to get information from private parties, but only with limitations. Under the currently in-force executive order, for example, OMB must invite an agency representative to meetings where that information is provided and must forward any information it receives to the agency, which must then place that information on the public record. OMB must also docket the fact that such meetings took place.

Here, the facts are not clear whether these requirements were satisfied (although the fact that the disclosures came in a newspaper article suggest that they were not). Nevertheless, even if there were violations, GB could not rely on them in its lawsuit. The executive orders in effect since the 1990s have made clear that the procedures entailed in those orders do not create rights that can be enforced by courts. Of course, GB might be able to attack the rulemaking process itself and use these violations as evidence of why the process was flawed. But the violations themselves do not state a claim for reversing the agency's action.

3. *Ex Parte* Contacts: Section 557(d) of the APA prohibits the type of *ex parte* contact reflected in the facts (the cocktail party conversation). Section 557(d) restricts any "interested person outside the agency" from making such contacts. The lobbyists in this case would surely come under this definition. The statute restricts such persons from making any "*ex parte* communication relevant to the merits of the proceeding." The plea to find a resolution that everyone "could live with" certainly comes within that definition.

However, this provision of the APA applies only to formal agency action [see 5 U.S.C. §557(a)]. As noted earlier, this rulemaking would be conducted under informal processes. While some cases have imposed freestanding, non–APA-based restrictions on *ex parte* communications in rulemaking [see *Home Box Office v. FCC*, 567 F.2d 9 (D.C. Cir. 1977)], other cases have largely limited that precedent [*e.g.*, *Action for Children's TV v. FCC*, 564 F.2d 458 (D.C. Cir. 1977)]. These other cases are generally considered to have stated the correct rule. Thus, the *ex parte* communications here would not furnish a ground for attacking the rule.

B. Substantive Claims

1. Statutory Interpretation: The first claim would be that the agency misread the statute. Before getting to the merits of the claim, the first question would be the level of deference that the agency would enjoy. The rule from *United States v. Mead Corp.*, 533 U.S. 218 (2001) is that, in general, if the agency is given power to act via rulemaking, and it interprets the statute while exercising that power, then *Chevron* deference is appropriate. Here, these conditions are satisfied; thus, most likely the agency's interpretation would receive *Chevron* deference.

Under *Chevron*, if the statute is clear on the precise issue in question, then the court simply applies that clear meaning. If the statute is not clear, then the court would uphold any reasonable interpretation the agency offered. In applying Step 1 of this test, a court can use "traditional tools of statutory construction," including sources such as text, legislative history, the overall structure of the statute and its relationship to other statutes, and canons of statutory interpretation.

Applying *Chevron*, the issue at hand is whether the statute gives the agency authority to prohibit certain substances in exercise drugs. The statute probably would be considered not to clearly answer that question; the authority in the statute is certainly broad, but the text does not address precisely whether that authority extends to prohibiting substances.

The canons from *Thompson*'s probably don't make the statute any clearer. Canon 4.10 suggests that the authority should not be read that broadly, while Canon 8.7 points in the other direction.

The only other guidance provided is in the statute itself, particularly in its findings. But those findings — in particular, the finding that exercise drugs can be beneficial — do not address the precise question of whether those drugs should or should not contain particular substances.

Given all this, a court would probably go to Step 2 of *Chevron* and ask if the agency gave a reasonable interpretation of the statute. This is generally considered a fairly lenient test; in general, so long as the agency gave some thought to the interpretive question and came up with a reasonable result, a court would uphold the result. Here, the agency's analysis of the events motivating Congress to act, and of Congress's findings, probably satisfy this relatively deferential standard. The fact that one of the interpretive canons points in this direction probably makes the agency's interpretation even more likely to be upheld under *Chevron* Step 2.

2. Policy Making: GB could also claim that the agency was arbitrary and capricious in its analysis of the regulatory issue. Agency actions taken via informal procedures, such as informal rulemaking, are subject to reversal if they are "arbitrary and capricious" (APA Section 706). Generally, this standard requires that the agency consider all the relevant factors and not to have made a clear error in judgment [*e.g.*, *Motor Veh. Mfrs Assn v. State Farm Mut. Ins. Co.*, 463 U.S. 29 (1983)]. Sometimes, this review is characterized as requiring that agencies take "a hard look" at its regulatory options. The materials set forth two reasons that the agency's action might fail this test.

First, GB could argue that the agency's depreciation method was arbitrary. The problem doesn't give any details about the agency's decision except the agency's statement that the depreciation method that it used is the one most commonly used in the United States. GB concedes that fact. That may not be a bad reason; still, it's a little perfunctory. If that is all the agency said, and if there is a good reason that that method does not correspond to the practices of this particular industry, then GB might have a good argument on this point.

Second, GB could argue that its own product is not carcinogenic. Again, the agency has a response — that such claims are unproven, and, until they are proven, it prefers to err on the side of caution. Unless GB can provide strong evidence that this is simply wrong, or that the agency ignored GB's proof, the agency's decision to err on the side of caution will probably be upheld. GB's argument that nobody has even gotten sick from its product is probably insufficient to strike down the agency's action unless that argument is supported with clinical proof, which the question indicates GB does not possess.

Thus, GB's best hope would be to argue that the agency's action was arbitrary and capricious on the depreciation point.

QUESTION #2

The issue would be whether the Department gave Ned an adequate hearing, consistent with due process. To succeed on this claim, Ned would have to show:

1. That he had a liberty or property interest;
2. That he was "deprived" of that interest; and
3. That he was not granted constitutionally adequate process before that deprivation.

1. Liberty or Property Interest?   Ned probably had a property interest in his job. A property interest is created when government gives someone a reasonable expectation that he or she will continue to enjoy a benefit if he or she meets certain criteria [*Bd of Regents v. Roth*, 408 U.S. 564 (1972)]. Even though Ned only signed year-to-year contracts, the tradition of longtime employment at the Department, plus the statement in the employee manual, would probably give him a reasonable expectation of continued employment, so long as he satisfied the criteria (which, of course, he wants a hearing to demonstrate). A similar situation arose in *Perry v. Sinderman*, 408 U.S. 593, (1972), where such a statement and a long-term course of dealing was held to justify a hearing on whether a property interest existed.

2. *Deprivation:* A negligent action by the government may not deprive one of a property interest [*Daniels v. Williams*, 474 U.S. 327 (1986)]. However, in this case, the deprivation was intentional, as the Department acted purposefully in firing Ned.

3. *Adequate Process:* In *Mathews v. Eldridge*, 424 U.S. 319 (1976), the Court laid down a three-part balancing test to judge the adequacy of the procedure afforded an individual. The test balances:

(1)   the importance of the interest to the class of recipients;
(2)   the risk of error in the current procedures and the possibility of improved accuracy if more procedure is provided; and
(3)   the government's interest.

(1) Importance of the Interest: This factor will not weigh overly strongly in Ned's favor. Note that what he is losing here is his salary during the pendency of an oral hearing, which might take so long as six months. He will also not get back pay should he win his appeal. While a salary is important, middle managers will probably be thought to have options that keep them from destitution should they be fired. Moreover, they may be presumed to have savings or other safety nets to cushion any shock. By contrast, in *Goldberg v. Kelly*, 397 U.S. 254 (1970), the Court noted that welfare benefits, as designed for people who are otherwise destitute, were extremely important to that class.

(2) Risk of Error and Possibility of Improvement: The difference here is between a decision made on a paper record and one made after an oral hearing. Depending on the basis for the action, a paper record may or may not be prone to erroneous decisions, and an oral hearing may or may not increase accuracy. For example, in *Goldberg*, the Court required an oral hearing, but in *Mathews*, the Court did not. *Mathews* reasoned that the issue in that case — whether the claimant was disabled — could be made easily based on medical records, and that an oral hearing wouldn't add much accuracy, while noting that in *Goldberg*, the Court was considering a decision to terminate welfare benefits, which turned on criteria that could be best determined through oral testimony.

In this case, it's unclear what the precise criteria are. However, presumably employment reviews would account for most of the relevant criteria, since that's what they're designed to do. Thus, it's unclear whether an oral hearing would add much accuracy. On the other hand, the very vagueness of the criteria that are provided ("happy and productive and an asset to the Department") suggests that oral testimony about Ned's attitude and general productiveness could conceivably be useful. The question is whether such information would normally not be conveyed in the written performance reviews. It's at least possible that, for example, coworker testimony could add information that is not provided in the written reviews.

(3) Government's Interest: In this case, the government's interest would mainly be to avoid the expense of paying the salary during the pendency of the oral hearing. Moreover, if the Department suspected Ned of malfeasance, it might be problematic for it to have him working, where he could potentially harm the Department more — although this could be taken care of by suspending Ned on full pay.

However, it should be noted that at least in some cases, the Supreme Court has considered the government's interest in a more expansive way. For example, in *Cleveland Bd of Education v. Loudermill*, 470 U.S. 532 (1985), another government employment case, the Court considered the government's interest to include an interest in retaining good workers. This would cut in *favor* of additional process.

Conclusion: On balance, these factors, especially 1 and 2, probably tip against Ned unless he could make a strong argument that the testimony of coworkers and others would establish that he satisfied the criteria for retaining his job (which would make Factor 2 swing in the opposite direction). Unless he could make such a showing, he will lose his procedural due process claim.

ADMINISTRATIVE LAW ESSAY EXAM #2

QUESTION #1

1. One potential constitutional issue is with the statute's requirement that regulations be transmitted to Congress 60 days before their effective date. One might think that this presents an issue of a potential legislative veto of the agency's regulations [see *INS v. Chadha*, 462 U.S. 919 (1983)]. However, the statute does not provide for an actual legislative veto of the regulations. Presumably, the 60-day period is intended to give Congress the time to stop a regulation before it becomes effective. However, Congress has the power to do this, so long as it does so by enacting a full-blown statute — *i.e.*, a law that satisfies bicameralism and presentment. Another conceivable reason is that the delay would allow time for Congress to impose informal pressure on the agency to rescind the regulation before its effective date. Neither of these possible congressional responses is unconstitutional.

2. One issue is procedural: whether the final agency regulation was the "logical outgrowth" of the proposed rule. This rule exists because otherwise, private parties would not have a real opportunity to comment on the agency's proposal since the final rule would, by hypothesis, not be closely related to the original proposal on which comment was solicited. See *Natural Resources Defense Council v. U.S. EPA*, 279 F.3d 1180 (9th Cir. 2002), applying this test.

Here, the question is whether the fireplace rule was the logical outgrowth of the original proposed rule. The change appears to have been from a rule about home heating and cooling efficiency to one that banned new fireplaces. This surely seems like a significant change in the agency's direction, from efficiency requirements to banning one type of heating system entirely. There is a good argument that the new rule was not a logical outgrowth of the old rule, and that, therefore, the agency violated the APA when it failed to reopen the comment period. Indeed, the agency notes that it did not receive any information contradicting its own study about fireplaces; it is at least possible that this was the case because the proposed regulation did not suggest that fireplaces (as opposed to heating systems more generally) were going to be the particular target of the regulation.

3. A second procedural violation may have occurred in the agency's failure to disclose the technical data relevant to the proposed regulation. It is true that the format through which commenters requested that data — interrogatories — were not part of the process that the agency had to follow. The agency did not have to follow formal rulemaking requirements because the statute did not use the "magic words" ("on the record after opportunity for agency hearing") required before such formality will be imposed [*Florida East Coast RR v. United States*, 410 U.S. 224 (1973)].

Nevertheless, the agency's failure to disclose this information probably violates the rule from *Nova Scotia Food Products Corp. v. United States*, 568 F.2d 240 (D.C. Cir. 1977), that such disclosure is necessary for the notice-and-comment process to be effective. The court's theory in that case was that disclosure of information important to the agency's decision-making process is necessary for parties to critique that decision making effectively. In turn, the lack of such disclosures essentially amounts to a denial of a meaningful opportunity to comment. Because this requirement is based on the explicit procedures set forth in the APA, it survives the Supreme Court's decision in *Vermont Yankee Nuclear Power Corp. v. Natural Resources Defense Council*, 435 U.S. 519 (1978), that courts should not impose their own freestanding conceptions of what additional procedures are appropriate for a given agency rulemaking.

4. The procedural failure noted in item 2, above, suggests that the regulation may have been arbitrary and capricious. Section 706 authorizes courts to set aside agency action found to be, among other things, arbitrary and capricious; this "arbitrary and capricious" standard applies to informal agency action, such as the rulemaking in this case. This standard generally requires the agency to consider the relevant factors and avoid making clear errors in judgment. It must also make its reasoning process relatively clear and consider all the major aspects of the regulatory problem confronting it [*Motor Vehicle Mfrs Ass'n v. State Farm Ins. Co.*, 463 U.S. 29 (1983)].

Here, the agency has arguably violated these requirements. The agency concluded that there was no way to increase fireplace efficiency. However, its failure to make clear to the regulated community that a fireplace ban was in the works quite likely led private parties not to critique the agency's conclusion. Thus, it's quite possible that the agency did not consider all the major aspects of the regulatory problem — for example, the problem of whether fireplaces could be made more efficient — largely because of its failure to seek out more information about the issue.

5. The final issue would be the agency's interpretation of the statutory term "unreasonable risk." Before getting to the merits of the claim, the first question would be the level of deference that the agency would enjoy. The rule from *United States v. Mead Corp.*, 533 U.S. 218 (2001) is that, in general, if the agency is given power to act via rulemaking, and it interprets the statute while exercising that power, then *Chevron* deference is appropriate. Here, these conditions are satisfied; thus, most likely the agency's interpretation would receive *Chevron* deference.

Under *Chevron*, if the statute is clear on the precise issue in question, then the court simply applies that clear meaning. If the statute is not clear, then the court would uphold any reasonable interpretation the agency offered. In applying Step 1 of this test, a court can use "traditional tools of statutory construction," including sources such as text, legislative history, the overall structure of the statute and its relationship to other statutes, and canons of statutory interpretation.

Here, the question is whether the statute clearly answers the interpretive question at issue. The statute's use of the term "unreasonable" probably suggests that it does not; almost as a matter of simple definition, "unreasonable" suggests the need to make judgment calls, which probably suggests some delegation of interpretive authority to the agency. Moreover, the statute's attempt to balance economic prosperity and environmental quality suggests that Congress did not settle on a precise policy path that would give the term "unreasonable risk" a definite meaning. For these reasons, the statute probably does not clearly answer the question, and a court would have to move on to *Chevron* Step 2.

Applying Step 2, it appears that the agency probably did act reasonably when it interpreted the statutory term the way it did. Its analysis is supported by references to both everyday and legal definitions of the concept of "unreasonableness." Its definition is also at least arguably supportive of Congress's intent to take a stand against climate change, especially in light of the fact that, given the current state of science, we do not know if small amounts of climate change will cause a "tipping point" at which a great deal of damage might be caused. Finally, the findings suggest a concern that U.S. actions set an example for the rest of the world; this concern also supports the agency's decision to combat even trivial sources of climate change, so long as those sources do not otherwise contribute significantly to Americans' standard of living. The agency explains all this, which further supports the reasonableness of its interpretation.

For these reasons, the agency's interpretation will probably be upheld under Step 2.

QUESTION #2

Several claims could be made against the regulation.

1. Rulemaking Process: Did the agency follow the correct rulemaking process? The first question is whether the agency should have used formal rulemaking processes, as was requested of and denied by the agency. This is clearly a case where only informal rulemaking is required. The statute's requirement that regulations be promulgated "after hearing" does not include the "magic words" ("on the record after an opportunity for agency hearing") required by *Florida East Coast RR v. United States*, 410 U.S. 224 (1973). Thus, only informal rulemaking, which does not require oral hearings or interrogatories, is called for.

During the 1960s and 1970s, some courts imposed more requirements than those imposed by the APA. The Supreme Court, however, in *Vermont Yankee Nuclear Power Co. v. Natural Resources Defense Council*, 435 U.S. 519 (1978), made clear that this was illegitimate; thus, a court would reject the claim that the importance of the issue requires additional procedures beyond those set forth in the APA.

2. Intra-Agency Discussions: The APA's rulemaking procedures do not prohibit the type of *ex parte* contacts noted here — *i.e.*, intra-agency contacts. Section 557(d) prohibits *ex parte* contacts involving persons *outside* the agency, but even there this prohibition applies only to formal rulemaking, not notice-and-comment rulemaking. Section 554(d) restricts intra-agency communications of this sort, but it applies only to *adjudications* (and only formal ones, at that).

In *Home Box Office, Inc. v. FCC*, 567 F.2d 9 (D.C. Cir. 1977), the appellate court did impose restrictions on *ex parte* contacts in rulemaking, but only contacts with personnel outside the agency. And even the *HBO* rule is generally considered not to be good law today, or at least of very limited applicability [see *Action for Children's TV v. FCC*, 564 F.2d 458 (D.C. Cir. 1977)]. Certainly, *Vermont Yankee, supra.*, suggests that *HBO* should not be read broadly.

Thus, the contacts noted in the research results are probably not violations of the APA.

3. Statutory Interpretation: Navarro could claim that the agency misread the statute. Before getting to the merits of the claim, the first question would be the level of deference that the agency would enjoy. The rule from *United States v. Mead Corp.*, 533 U.S. 218 (2001) is that, in general, if the agency is given power to act via rulemaking, and it interprets the statute while exercising that power, then *Chevron* deference is appropriate. Here, these conditions are satisfied; thus, most likely the agency's interpretation would receive *Chevron* deference.

Under *Chevron*, if the statute is clear on the precise issue in question, then the court simply applies that clear meaning. If the statute is not clear, then the court would uphold any reasonable interpretation the agency offered. In applying Step 1 of this test, a court can use "traditional tools of statutory construction," including sources such as text, legislative history, the overall structure of the statute and its relationship to other statutes, and canons of statutory interpretation.

Applying *Chevron*, the issue at hand is the definition of "employee," and whether it includes issues of federal law immigration status. The statute probably would be considered not to clearly answer that question. The canon from *Thompson's* probably doesn't make the statute any clearer; it doesn't cut against the agency's position, but it doesn't make the agency's position a clear winner, either.

But even if a court found the statute not clear, the agency would probably win at Step 2 of *Chevron*. This is generally considered a fairly lenient test; in general, so long as the agency gave some thought to the interpretive question and came up with a reasonable result, a court would uphold the result.

First, the agency explained that its choice was based on the interpretive canon requiring that every word in the statute be given meaning. This helps make its interpretive choice appear reasonable. Of course, commenters pointed out that other interpretations would also satisfy this goal, but if the statute is ambiguous, then all that's necessary is for the agency's choice to be reasonable, not that it be the best choice.

Second, the agency explained that its interpretive choice placed its policy in sync with the President's overall policy agenda (here, that all agencies should worry, within their spheres of competence, about homeland security). *Chevron* explicitly contemplates that an agency may make an interpretive choice based on this consideration, so long as that choice is reasonable.

Third, the agency's rejection of the "congressional ratification" argument also appears appropriate under *Chevron*. Again, *Chevron* accepts an agency changing its interpretive choices to make them more consistent with the President's overall agenda. This suggests that so long as the new interpretation is reasonable, the fact that it shifts direction should not cut against it. (Note that this is different from *Skidmore* deference where, among other factors, the consistency of the agency's interpretation is one factor in determining how much deference it is due.)

Here, the agency's dictionary-based interpretation would most likely at least be found reasonable (at Step 2 of *Chevron*), and might even reflect the clear meaning of the statute (at Step 1).

4. The Hearing Procedure: The ALJ conducted only a paper hearing, denying Navarro the right to call witnesses. This conflicts with the APA's procedures for formal adjudications, set forth at Sections 556 and 557 of the APA.

This fact raises the question whether such a formal adjudication was required here. The statute states that adjudications shall be conducted "on the record, after opportunity for agency hearing." This is precisely the language that triggers the formal adjudication requirements of the APA. See APA Section 556 (a), noting that the requirements of Section 556, and by extension, 557, apply when the agency acts in accordance with Section 554(a); in turn, Section 554(a) is triggered when adjudications are required to be conducted "on the record after opportunity for an agency hearing.") Thus, this hearing should have been conducted pursuant to the formal adjudication requirements of Sections 556 and 557, which give the right to oral testimony.

ADMINISTRATIVE LAW ESSAY EXAM #3

QUESTION #1

Question 1: Reviewability, Agency Action, Jurisdiction

The issues that Hal might be able to raise are procedural due process, and whether the agency misread the statute when it interpreted the phrase "actually dependent." Question 1 asks whether these claims could be raised in a lawsuit in federal court. The main issues raised here are reviewability, agency action, and jurisdiction.

1. Reviewability: Sections 701–706 of the APA provide the guidelines for judicial review of agency action. Section 701 states that these sections apply except to the extent that "statutes preclude judicial review" or "agency action is committed to agency discretion by law."

The APA has been interpreted as enacting a presumption that judicial review is available [*e.g., Block v. Community Nutrition Institute,* 467 U.S. 340 (1984)]. The Supreme Court has also described these two exceptions to judicial review as "narrow." See *Citizens to Preserve Overton Park v. Volpe,* 401 U.S. 402 (1971).

The first of these exceptions might be seen as preventing judicial review in this case. After all, Section 4 of the statute seems to so state. However, courts have found creative ways of reading these statutes so as not to preclude judicial review. In particular, courts have read statutes precluding review of particular decisions that agencies make when administering programs (such as the one in Section 4 here) as not precluding review of broader, more general, challenges to agency action. See, *e.g., Bowen v. Michigan Academy of Family Physicians,* 476 U.S. 667 (1986); and *DeMore v. Kim,* 538 U.S. 510 (2003). The claims that Hal might make here — that the agency misread the statute and that its regulations violate due process — are broad challenges to the agency's conduct rather than narrow challenges to the particular decisions that the agency reaches in applying standards and procedures that a plaintiff concedes are legally valid. While the statute might well be read to preclude challenges of the latter sort, challenges of the former type might well be allowed, especially in light of the presumption in favor of judicial review.

This conclusion is strengthened by the fact that both of these challenges have at least some constitutional foundation. Obviously, the due process claim is constitutional, and the statutory interpretation claim has a constitutional backdrop to it, to the extent that Hal might argue that the interpretation unconstitutionally discriminates against the type of relationship he has with his child. See, *e.g., Webster v. Doe,* 486 U.S. 592 (1988), noting that there would be a "serious constitutional question" raised if a statute precluded judicial review of a colorable constitutional claim. For these reasons, the statute would probably not be read to preclude judicial review of Hal's claims.

The second exception, for "agency action committed to agency discretion by law," is easier to resolve. This is a narrow exception that applies only when the statute is written so broadly that there is "no law [for a court] to apply" [*Citizens to Preserve Overton Park v. Volpe*, 401 U.S. 402 (1971)]. Here, the statute sets forth the "law" reasonably clearly, if not with complete precision: Dependents are eligible for the program if they are "actually dependent" on the veteran. This is enough of a legal standard to satisfy this requirement.

2. Agency Action: Section 704 of the APA provides that persons may challenge "final agency action." To be final, (1) agency action must mark the consummation of the agency's decision-making process, and (2) the action must be one by which rights or obligations have been determined, or from which legal consequences will follow [*Bennett v. Spear*, 520 U.S. 154 (1997)]. Here, the agency's regulations, which set forth both the procedure that Hal is challenging and reflect the agency's statutory interpretation decision, clearly mark the consummation of the agency's decision-making processes on these questions. Moreover, they establish Hal's legal rights, both procedural and substantive. Thus, the "agency action" requirement is satisfied.

3. Jurisdiction: The APA does not confer jurisdiction. In this case, neither does the statute (unsurprisingly, since Congress purported to preclude judicial review, as noted above). However, jurisdiction could be based on the general federal question jurisdiction statute, 28 U.S.C. §1331, since Hal's challenges would clearly raise federal questions.

Question 2: Standing

The question asks whether Hal would have standing to sue to raise the claims identified above.

Standing to challenge agency action has both a constitutional component and a procedural one. The constitutional requirements are that the plaintiff (1) be injured, (2) in a way caused by the defendant, and that (3) the injury be redressable by a court.

1. Injury: Injury must be concrete, and actual or imminent rather than speculative and remote [*Lujan v. Defenders of Wildlife*, 504 U.S. 555 (1992)]. Here, the issue is whether the deprivation of free medical care to Diana would injure Hal. A court would probably hold that it would. Deprivation of that care might well lead to Hal incurring expenses for Diana's medical care. Of course, it might be argued that Hal would be under no legal obligation to provide such care; however, it's probably fairly easy for a court to conclude that a father would likely pay, or attempt to pay, for his daughter's care, especially where, as here, the divorce was amicable and Hal appears willing to shoulder part of the cost of raising Diana. It might also be argued that there's no guarantee that Diana would in fact incur medical expenses. Again, though, it's likely that she would, given the common knowledge that children often incur medical issues. If nothing else, routine vaccinations are certainly predictable and would require a payout of money. Finally, at the very least, deprivation of this free care would likely lead her parents to seek to cover Diana under private medical insurance, which would require expenditures.

2. Causation: This is easy to meet, since the injury described above is caused by the agency's statutory interpretation. The procedural due process claim is a bit more complicated, but not much: At the very least, Hal would have to pay for

Diana's care temporarily during the pendency of the appeals process. This injury would be caused by the fact that, according to him, his due process rights require a more elaborate procedure earlier in the process. The failure to provide such a procedure, or the failure to continue to pay benefits during the appeals process (which is essentially the same claim) would require an outlay of funds, at least until the government reimbursed Hal. (Note also that the regulations allow for reimbursement of "reasonable and necessary" expenses, which might mean that Hal would not get fully reimbursed even if he wins his appeal under the current process.)

3. Redressability: Again, this is easy to meet. If the regulations are struck down, Hal's injury will be redressed.

4. Zone of Interests: The prudential standing requirement applicable here is that the plaintiff be "arguably within the zone of interests sought to be protected by the statute" [*Association of Data Processing Service Organizations v. Camp*, 397 U.S. 150 (1970)]. This language is an interpretation of APA Section 702, which grants parties "adversely affected or aggrieved by agency action within the meaning of the relevant statute" the right to sue. This is an easy test to meet. Here, Hal's status as a veteran clearly places him within the zone of interests since the statute was likely drafted exactly to benefit people like him.

Thus, Hal would likely have standing to sue.

Question 3: The Merits Arguments

Hal could probably make a procedural due process argument against the regulations, as well as an argument that the agency misread the statute when it defined "actually dependent" in the manner it did.

1. Procedural Due Process: Due process requires inquiries into three issues: (1) Is there a life, liberty or property interest; (2) has there been a deprivation; and (3) has a sufficient amount of process been provided?

a. *Existence of the Interest:* Here, the only likely type of interest that Hal would have would be a property interest. Property interests are not created by the Constitution; rather, their existence is determined by asking whether the plaintiff had an objectively reasonable expectation of the benefit, based on some legal source other than the Constitution—*i.e.*, state law or sub-constitutional federal law [*Bd of Regents v. Roth*, 408 U.S. 564 (1972)]. Here, the statute, which makes Hal eligible for the Program if he meets certain criteria (*i.e.*, having a dependent who is actually dependent on him), provides that expectation. Thus, Hal would have a property interest in eligibility for the Program.

b. *Deprivation:* Deprivations of due process interests must be intentional for the due process guarantee to apply; mere negligent "deprivation" is insufficient [*Daniels v. Williams*, 474 U.S. 327 (1986)]. Here, the deprivation is clearly intentional, in the sense that the agency is consciously depriving Diana of eligibility for the Program. Thus, this requirement is satisfied.

c. *Sufficiency of the Process Provided:* In *Mathews v. Eldridge*, 424 U.S. 319 (1976), the Court announced a three-factor test to determine how much process is constitutionally due. In making this determination, a court must consider (1) the importance of the private interest, applied to the entire class of beneficiaries; (2) the lack of accuracy inherent in the current procedures used, and the increased accuracy to be expected from the procedures requested; and (3) the government's interest.

The first of these factors asks how important continued program eligibility is to the class of veterans and their dependents during the pendency of the appeals. As the facts state, it could be 12 months until Hal gets an oral hearing, and the oral hearing process begins only after he loses the first appeal, the time frame of which is not set forth in the materials. Even though Hal may ultimately recoup his costs (at least if they are "reasonable and necessary"), he would, at the least, have to incur these expenses during the pendency of his appeal.

How significant is this deprivation? It's obviously hard to know with precision. Unlike the program in *Goldberg v. Kelly*, 397 U.S. 254 (1970), the program here is not predicated on the assumption that the recipient is needy; that is, any veteran is eligible, regardless of his or her financial situation. On the other hand, it's probably fair to say that many veterans are not wealthy, and that the need to pay for medical expenses can be significant.

The second factor is also somewhat tricky. If it weren't for the exception for compelling circumstances, it's probably the case that the current procedures are quite accurate in making eligibility determinations because eligibility turns on a simple, easily provable fact of the existence of a legal relationship between the veteran and the child. Thus, a pre-termination oral hearing of the type Hal wants probably wouldn't increase accuracy very much.

However, the existence of the "compelling circumstances" exception to the legal status requirement opens the door for the argument that an oral hearing would increase decisional accuracy because the decision maker could hear the parties state their case about why their situation is different from the norm. The force of this argument is mitigated somewhat by the agency's insistence that this exception is quite narrow. The import of that fact is that relatively few decisions will be changed based on a finding of compelling circumstances — or, to put it differently, decisions based on a paper hearing will remain relatively accurate. Still, the existence of this exception to noneligibility makes this element cut more strongly in favor of Hal's claim.

The final factor is the government's interest, which is normally understood as its interest in avoiding administrative costs and program costs. There probably won't be much of an increase in administrative costs: To the extent that all claimants eventually seek an oral hearing, ALJs will have to be paid either way. But it's possible that under the current process, some (maybe many) claimants will drop their appeals before that point; however, if oral hearings are provided before a cutoff decision is made, claimants will have an incentive to invoke those hearings, if only to keep the benefits flowing during the pendency of the oral hearing process. Moreover, if the demand for such hearings is high and the backlog becomes intolerable, the government may have to hire more ALJs.

Still, the most significant part of this factor is probably the costs of providing health care during the pendency of the oral hearing. As noted above, the existence of a pre-termination oral hearing would probably prompt most claimants to invoke that right, if only to keep the benefits flowing during the oral hearing process. The statute does not provide for the government recouping costs found to be paid out in error, so if lots of claimants invoked the oral hearing and were still found not eligible, the cost to the government of providing the pre-termination hearing could be significant.

In sum, these factors probably cut in favor of pre-termination oral hearings, though the lack of clarity about the size of the "compelling circumstances" exception and the size of the monetary risks to the government could well lead a court to decide in the other direction.

2. Statutory Interpretation: Hal's other argument would be that the agency misread the statute when it read "actually dependent" as narrowly as it did.

Before getting to the merits of the claim, the first question would be the level of deference that the agency would enjoy. The rule from *United States v. Mead Corp.*, 533 U.S. 218 (2001) is that, in general, if the agency is given power to act via rulemaking and it interprets the statute while exercising that power, then *Chevron* deference is appropriate. Here, these conditions are satisfied; thus, most likely the agency's interpretation would receive *Chevron* deference.

Under *Chevron*, if the statute is clear on the precise issue in question, then the court simply applies that clear meaning. If the statute is not clear, then the court would uphold any reasonable interpretation offered by the agency. In applying Step 1 of this test, a court can use "traditional tools of statutory construction," including sources such as text, legislative history, the overall structure of the statute and its relationship to other statutes, and canons of statutory interpretation.

It is possible that the statute clearly answers the question whether "actually dependent" requires a legal relationship between the veteran and the dependent. "Actually" does have some sense of being different from "formally" or "legally," which is how the agency interpreted the term. Indeed, in some basic sense, "actually" suggests, literally, "actual" *de facto* dependence, a conclusion that cuts against the agency's interpretation. There are no other interpretive guides provided in the materials, and the agency provides relatively little analysis about what the words actually mean. It is possible that the agency could lose this argument at Step 1 of *Chevron*.

If a court finds the statute ambiguous, the agency still might lose. Again, the agency cites no authority for the proposition of what Congress really intended with this language. All the agency does say is that the interpretation accords with the President's larger agenda. This is certainly an allowable consideration under Step 2 of *Chevron*; however, without any other support for the reasonableness of the agency's interpretation, this might not be enough to carry the day.

Finally, it is unclear whether the constitutional issue raised by the agency's interpretation cuts against the agency's interpretation here. In *FCC v. Fox Television Stations*, 129 S. Ct. 1800 (2009), a five-justice majority on the Court suggested that this factor would not cut against the agency's interpretation, although in that case the Court was engaged in arbitrary and capricious review, not review under Step 2 of *Chevron*. (Still, some have suggested that these two review approaches are very similar; if that is true, then *Fox*'s refusal to consider this factor might apply as well to a court's Step 2 analysis here.) At any rate, this factor cuts even further against the agency's interpretation; thus, if the agency's interpretation is already on shaky ground, this last factor, if it does anything at all, makes that ground even shakier.

In sum, it is quite possible that Hal could prevail on this claim, either under Step 1 or 2 of *Chevron*.

QUESTION #2

1. Informal Rulemaking: The APA does not restrict *ex parte* communications when the agency is engaging in informal, notice-and-comment, rulemaking. In *Home Box Office, Inc. v. FCC*, 567 F.2d 9 (D.C. Cir. 1977), the appellate court did impose restrictions on *ex parte* contacts in rulemaking, but only contacts with personnel outside the agency. And even the *HBO* rule is generally considered not to be good law today, or at least of very limited applicability. See *Action for Children's TV v. FCC*, 564 F.2d 458 (D.C. Cir. 1977). This is especially the case after *Vermont Yankee Nuclear Power Corp. v. Natural Resources Defense Council*, 435 U.S. 519 (1978), held that courts could not use their own freestanding conceptions of how much process an agency should use when engaging in rulemaking.

Based on this law, it is clear that the decision maker could have the conversation with the agency technical expert.

The discussion with the lobbyist presents a slightly more difficult question. *HBO* condemned *ex parte* contacts with personnel outside the agency. However, as noted above, *HBO* has been read in a limited way. In particular, that case has been read to limit such contacts only when there is involved "resolution of conflicting private claims to a valuable privilege" [*Action for Children's TV v. FCC*, 564 F.2d 458 (D.C. Cir. 1977)]. The classic example of such a situation is where the Federal Communications Commission (FCC), by regulation, awards a broadcast license to a particular party [see *Sangamon Valley Television Corp. v. United States*, 269 F.2d 221 (D.C. Cir. 1959)]. The idea here is that when a rulemaking resembles an adjudication, in that it essentially resolves which party will receive a valuable privilege, more guarantees against external *ex parte* contacts may be appropriate.

Here, we don't know the subject of the rulemaking. For that reason, we can't know for sure if *HBO*, in its more truncated version, governs, or whether the case will be governed by the default rule allowing such contacts.

2. Formal Rulemaking: As with informal rulemaking, the APA does not proscribe intra-agency *ex parte* contacts. Thus, again there is no problem with the agency decision maker speaking with the agency expert.

However, Section 557(d) of the APA does prohibit an agency decision maker from speaking with interested persons *outside* the agency about a matter relevant to the decision making. This restriction applies to formal rulemaking [see Section 557(d)]. Thus, the discussion with the lobbyist would be prohibited. The lobbyist is clearly an interested person, and the facts state that the discussion featured the lobbyist's arguments relative to the merits of the decision. Thus, this discussion would be illegal.

3. Formal Adjudication: Section 554(d) of the APA restricts the ability of agency decision makers to confer confidentially even with personnel inside the agency. Indeed, the relevant language restricts ALJs from discussing relevant matters with "a person or party on a fact in issue." However, when the agency decision-maker is the agency head rather than an ALJ, this restriction does not apply. Nevertheless, Section 557(d) would continue to restrict *ex parte* contacts with persons *outside* the agency, even when the decision maker is the agency head. This law allows us to answer the questions.

With regard to the discussion with the agency expert, if the decision maker was an ALJ, then that discussion could not take place [see Section 554(d)]. If the decision-maker was an agency head, then that discussion would be legal since, again, Section 554(d) exempts agency heads from the rule governing ALJs.

With regard to the discussion with the lobbyist, if the decision maker was an ALJ, then he or she would be prohibited from engaging in that conversation, both because of Section 554(d) and 557(d). If the decision maker was the agency head, then Section 554(d) would not restrict it, but 557(d) would still apply and make that discussion illegal.

ADMINISTRATIVE LAW ESSAY EXAM #4

QUESTION #1

A. Can the Association Sue?

1. Jurisdiction: Jurisdiction in a federal court would present no problem. The APA itself does not confer jurisdiction to sue an agency. In this case, neither does the statute under which the agency is acting. However, the association could invoke a court's general federal question jurisdiction, 28 U.S.C. §1331, which would suffice to establish jurisdiction.

2. Reviewability: The first issue here is reviewability. There is a presumption that agency action is reviewable [*e.g.*, *Block v. Community Nutrition Institute*, 467 U.S. 340 (1984), noting this presumption]. The exceptions — for preclusion by statute and for action committed to agency discretion by law — do not apply here. First, the statute says nothing about precluding judicial review. Second, the standard for action committed to agency discretion by law — whether the statute is written so broadly that there is "no law to apply" — is clearly not met here, *i.e.*, the statute clearly provides a sufficient legal standard that a court could apply. Compare *Citizens to Preserve Overton Park v. Volpe*, 401 U.S. 402 (1971), finding the statute there similarly definite. Thus, this action is reviewable.

3. Standing: The next question is whether the association has standing. Standing has both a constitutional and a prudential component. Standing has a special set of rules when an association is suing on behalf of its members.

Associational standing: For an association to have standing, it must meet three requirements. First, at least one member must have standing to sue. Second, the subject of the lawsuit must be germane to the association's purposes. Third, the relief sought must be effective in the absence of the injured member as a named party [*Hunt v. Washington State Apple Advertising Comm'n*, 432 U.S. 333 (1977)].

Whether one member would have standing is considered below. The second prong is satisfied because, as noted in the facts, the association (unsurprisingly) exists to promote the interests of cattle ranchers, who are of course affected by this law. The third prong is satisfied because, again as noted in the facts, the goal of the lawsuit is to get the regulation struck down. This type of injunctive relief is generally considered the appropriate type of relief for an association to sue, compared, say, to damages, which a court would not be able to ensure flowed to the injured party.

Would an individual member have standing?

Constitutional standing: Article III requires that a plaintiff (1) be injured, (2) that the injury be caused by the defendant, and (3) that the injury be redressable by a court. The injury must be concrete, and either actual or imminent [*Lujan v. Defenders of Wildlife*, 504 U.S. 555 (1992)]. Here, a member would be clearly injured by the agency's action, which will affect its business operations and profits. The injury is at least imminent, given the promulgation of the regulation. It is also caused by the agency, and an injunction against the regulation would redress its injury.

Prudential standing: Section 702 of the APA has been interpreted to impose a prudential standing bar that the plaintiff be "arguably within the zone of interests sought to be protected by the statute" [*Assn of Data Processing Serv. Organizations v. Camp*, 397 U.S. 150 (1970)]. This is a very lenient test to meet, and a rancher-member would surely meet it. The statute itself notes the benefits of food additives in encouraging consumption, and the statute's caution in not banning all food additives suggests at least some concern for food producers, thus bringing a producer like a rancher within the zone.

Thus, a member would satisfy both constitutional and prudential requirements for standing. For that reason, the first prong of the *Washington Apple* test is satisfied, and thus the association would have standing.

4. Timing of Judicial Review: Timing in this context implicates two issues: finality and ripeness.

Finality: APA Section 704 requires that an agency action be final before it is subject to judicial review. To be final, (1) agency action must mark the consummation of the agency's decision-making process, and (2) the action must be one by which rights or obligations have been determined, or from which legal consequences will follow [*Bennett v. Spear*, 520 U.S. 154 (1997)]. Here, promulgation of a regulation would satisfy these requirements: It clearly marks the culmination of the agency's rulemaking process, and the ensuing rule creates legal obligations for ranchers. Thus, the action is final.

Ripeness: The final question is whether the association's lawsuit would be ripe. The general rule is that pre-enforcement review of an agency regulation is allowed so long as the issue is appropriate for judicial resolution in the absence of further factual developments, and the private party would face hardship if it had to wait for the agency to commence an enforcement action before it could sue [*Abbott Labs v. Gardner*, 387 U.S. 136 (1967)]. Here, the purely legal issues surrounding the rule are clearly amenable to judicial resolution at this early phase. Moreover, the harm that ranchers would face — the economic uncertainty affecting their decisions about the amount of beef to start producing — is significant, even if it doesn't rise to the level of, say, a criminal sanction. Thus, the association's challenge would probably be ripe.

B. Claims on the Merits
Procedural Claims

1. Formal v. Informal Rulemaking: This is clearly a case where only informal rulemaking is required. The statute does not even come close to the "magic words" ("on the record after opportunity for agency hearing") required by *Florida East Coast RR v. United States*, 410 U.S. 224 (1973). Thus, only informal rulemaking, which does not require oral hearings or interrogatories, is called for.

During the 1960s and 1970s, some courts imposed more requirements than those imposed by the APA. However, the Supreme Court in *Vermont Yankee Nuclear Power Co. v. Natural Resources Defense Council*, 435 U.S. 519 (1978), made clear that this was illegitimate; thus, a court would reject the claim that the importance of the issue requires additional procedures beyond those set forth in the APA.

2. OMB Approval: Executive orders in effect since the 1990s generally do not absolutely require that an agency get OMB approval before promulgating a regulation; instead, usually the process is a consultative one between OMB and the agency. But regardless of any ambiguity on this issue, these orders have consistently provided that the procedures entailed in those orders do not create rights that can be enforced by courts. Thus, any violations do not state a claim for reversing the agency's action in court.

3. Ex Parte Contacts: The APA's rulemaking procedures do not prohibit the type of *ex parte* contacts noted here, that is, intra-agency contacts. Section 557(d) prohibits *ex parte* contacts involving persons *outside* the agency, but even there, this prohibition applies only to formal rulemaking, not notice-and-comment rulemaking. Section 554(d) restricts intra-agency communications of this sort, but it applies only to *adjudications* (and only formal ones, at that).

In *Home Box Office, Inc. v. FCC*, 567 F.2d 9 (D.C. Cir. 1977), the appellate court did impose restrictions on *ex parte* contacts in rulemaking, but only contacts with personnel outside the agency. And even the *HBO* rule is generally considered not to be good law today, or at least of very limited applicability [see *Action for Children's TV v. FCC*, 564 F.2d 458 (D.C. Cir. 1977)]. Certainly, *Vermont Yankee* suggests that *HBO* should not be read broadly.

Thus, the contacts noted in the newspaper article are probably not violations of the APA.

4. Failure to Disclose: However, the association may have a good procedural claim based on the agency's failure to provide the public with its toxicological assumptions during the rulemaking process. In cases such as *Nova Scotia Food Products Corp. v. United States*, 568 F.2d 240 (D.C. Cir. 1977), courts have read the notice-and-comment procedure so as to require agencies to disclose their main assumptions and the support for their assumptions, on the theory that there is no real chance to comment if parties don't know the technical bases for the agency's proposed rule. This principle survived *Vermont Yankee* because it is based on the APA's procedures rather than on judges' own free-floating ideas of what types of procedures are proper. The agency's failure to disclose this information in this case might well constitute a violation of *Nova Scotia*.

Substantive Claims

1. Statutory Interpretation: The first claim would be that the agency misread the statute. Before getting to the merits of the claim, the first question would be the level of deference that the agency would enjoy. The rule from *United States v. Mead Corp.*, 533 U.S. 218 (2001), is that, in general, if the agency is given power to act via rulemaking, and it interprets the statute while exercising that power, then *Chevron* deference is appropriate. Here, these conditions are satisfied; thus, most likely the agency's interpretation would receive *Chevron* deference.

Under *Chevron*, if the statute is clear on the precise issue in question, then the court simply applies that clear meaning. If the statute is not clear, then the court would uphold any reasonable interpretation offered by the agency. In applying Step 1 of this test, a court can use "traditional tools of statutory construction," including sources such as text, legislative history, the overall structure of the statute and its relationship to other statutes, and canons of statutory interpretation.

Applying *Chevron*, the issue at hand is the definition of "naturally occurring." The statute probably would be considered not to clearly answer that question. The canon from *Thompson*'s probably doesn't make the statute any clearer, though arguably it supports the agency's position. Still, one might argue that that canon supports the agency's meaning as a matter of the statute's precise meaning, since presumably the plain meaning of words would be found in a dictionary.

But even if a court found that the statute was not clear, the agency would probably win at Step 2 of *Chevron*. This is generally considered a fairly lenient test; in general, so long as the agency gave some thought to the interpretive question and came up with a reasonable result, a court would uphold the result. Here, the agency's dictionary-based interpretation most likely would at least be found reasonable (at Step 2 of *Chevron*), and might even reflect the clear meaning of the statute (at Step 1).

2. Policy Making: The association could also claim that the agency was arbitrary and capricious in its analysis of the regulatory issue. Agency action taken via informal procedures, such as informal rulemaking, are subject to reversal if they are "arbitrary and capricious" (APA Section 706). Generally, this standard requires that the agency to have considered all the relevant factors and not to have made a clear error of judgment [*e.g.*, *Motor Veh. Mfrs Assn v. State Farm Mut. Ins. Co.*, 463 U.S. 29 (1983)]. Sometimes, this review is characterized as requiring that agencies take "a hard look" at its regulatory options. The materials set forth two reasons that the agency's action might fail this test.

a. The Regulatory Threshold: The association could attack the agency's decision to use such a low risk threshold. However, the agency appears to have explained its position fairly thoroughly, both as a matter of deciding to err on the side of caution and also as a matter of noting that any excessive deterrence of beef consumption probably itself would help Americans' health. A court would likely reject an attack on this part of the agency's analysis.

b. The Consumption Assumptions: Again, the agency seems to have explained itself adequately, at least enough to beat back a claim that it acted arbitrarily and capriciously. The agency explained why more recent data would be either hard to find or biased. It also explained why the 2000 data was objective and likely to be reasonably accurate. Finally, again, it noted that any error would likely be on the side of over-deterring beef consumption, which, as noted above, the agency was probably reasonable in considering a collateral benefit of its action. It's not perfect—most notably, it's not clear that the agency had any business thinking about dietary health in general, as opposed to the health implications of food coloring. But that analysis was, if anything, a collateral benefit of its conclusion that more recent data would either be unavailable or unreliable. That conclusion would most likely survive judicial review under the arbitrary and capricious standard, though, as always, a stricter court might have some concerns with it.

Thus, GB's best hope would be to argue that the agency's action violated the procedural requirements of the APA.

QUESTION #2

Several basic FOIA principles would be relevant here.

1. FOIA enshrines a basic principle of government openness. Congress's basic goal in enacting the statute was to ensure private access to information in the government's possession. Thus, unless information comes within one of FOIA's exemptions, the default is that the government has a duty to disclose the information [*Dept of the Air Force v. Rose*, 425 U.S. 352 (1976)].

2. However, FOIA has a number of exemptions [5 U.S.C. §552(b)]. One exemption that might be relevant here would be exemption 6, for "personnel and medical files and similar files the disclosure of which would constitute a clearly unwarranted invasion of personal privacy." It might well be the case that disclosure of this information, at least with Howell's name on the files, would fall within this exception (*Rose*, dealing with a factually similar FOIA request).

3. The existence of exemptions does not mean that if material falls within an exemption, the agency is required to withhold it. Rather, because FOIA is a disclosure statute, the applicability of an exemption merely gives the agency the authority to withhold disclosure [*Chrysler Corp. v. Brown*, 441 U.S. 281 (1979)]. Thus, a party like Howell, who objects to disclosure, may not argue that applicability of a FOIA exemption mandates nondisclosure.

4. However, such a party could argue that the decision to disclose was arbitrary and capricious (*Chrysler*). Lawsuits where a party makes such an argument are known as "reverse-FOIA" suits since, rather than demanding disclosure, they challenge an agency's decision to disclose. Reverse-FOIA suits are allowed (*Chrysler*).

5. Sometimes a file or report may have information that is both subject to and exempt from disclosure. In a case like that, FOIA requires that "any reasonable segregable portion of a record shall be provided . . . after deletion of the portions which are exempt. . . ." [5 U.S.C. §552(b)].

6. When confronted with a FOIA suit and either resistance from the agency or a reverse-FOIA suit (or, as here, with both agency resistance and a reverse-FOIA suit), a question arises as to the method a court should use in resolving the dispute. In *Rose*, the Supreme Court held that courts must review *de novo* any decision to withhold information on the ground that disclosure is exempt under FOIA.

7. Judicial review in turn raises the question of how the court should go about determining whether particular information is exempt from disclosure. In *Rose*, the Court endorsed the practice of judges reviewing the disputed information in chambers to determine whether a FOIA exemption applied.

8. Finally, FOIA provides that "the court may assess against the United States reasonable attorney fees and other litigation costs reasonably incurred in any case . . . in which the complainant has substantially prevailed" [Section 552(a)(4)(E)].

> ## ADMINISTRATIVE LAW ESSAY EXAM #5

> ### QUESTION #1

1. Nondelegation: The first question is whether the statute is so broad that it violates the nondelegation doctrine. Article I of the Constitution vests "all legislative powers herein granted" in Congress, and for that reason, it has been interpreted to prohibit Congress from delegating its legislative power.

Of course, Congress cannot prescribe every detail of every policy; thus, the Court allows significant grants of quasi-legislative power to administrative agencies. The constitutional test for such delegations is whether the statute contains an "intelligible principle" [*J.W. Hampton Co. v. United States*, 276 U.S. 394 (1928)]. The Court has found this standard to have been violated only in two cases, *A.L.A. Schechter Poultry Corp. v. United States*, 295 U.S. 495 (1935); and *Panama Refining Co. v. Ryan*, 293 U.S. 388 (1935). Both of these cases dealt with exceptionally broad grants of power from Congress to regulate large parts of the economy. Since 1935, the Court has never struck down a statute as violating the nondelegation doctrine, even though statutes have been written very broadly [*e.g.*, *National Broadcasting Co. v. United States*, 319 U.S. 190 (1943), upholding delegation to the FCC to grant broadcast licenses "in the public interest"].

Here, the statutory delegation is far less sweeping. The grant of authority is limited to Internet transactions. The mandate is similarly limited, to ensure their maximum safety. The "to the extent feasible" language does suggest some degree of discretion on the part of the agency to decide how much regulation is in fact feasible. However, the amount of discretion granted appears well within the outer limits of delegations that the Court has allowed.

There is most likely no nondelegation violation in this statute.

2. Legislative Veto: The statute contains a legislative veto and is unconstitutional for that reason. A legislative veto is a provision in a statute that allows Congress to alter legal rights and duties by means short of bicameralism and presentment, and not otherwise provided for in the Constitution (for example, the Senate's power to advise and consent to presidential appointees). In *INS v. Chadha*, 462 U.S. 919 (1983), the Court struck down a provision that allowed one house of Congress to overrule deportation decisions made by the Attorney General, on the ground that it allowed Congress to change aliens' legal rights and duties by means short of bicameralism and presentment.

Here, the statute's provision for overturning regulations promulgated by the agency by majority votes of both houses of Congress constitutes a legislative veto because it lacks presentment to the President. There is no bicameralism problem here since both houses of Congress must approve the regulation revocation. But there is still a presentment problem, and for that reason, the provision constitutes a legislative veto and is unconstitutional under *Chadha*.

3. Appointment and Removal: The statute's appointment and removal provisions are also potentially problematic. Article II states that the President shall appoint "officers of the United States," but that Congress may vest the appointment of "inferior officers" in the President, the courts, or the heads of departments, as Congress sees fit. Thus, for appointment purposes, it doesn't matter whether the head of the agency is an officer of the United States or an inferior officer; either way, the statute is constitutional in its vesting of appointment power in the President.

The head of a department is probably an inferior officer, in light of the fact that he or she is subject to control by the head of a department (the Secretary of Commerce). The department head's policy-making power may also be considered at least somewhat limited, given the narrow scope of his or her authority under the statute [see *Morrison v. Olson*, 487 U.S. 654 (1988), discussing these criteria]. The principal–inferior officer distinction will become relevant later in this answer.

The removal provision, however, may be a problem. In *Morrison*, the Court rejected the argument that Article II requires the President to have complete removal authority over all inferior officers. The argument had been made that this broad authority was required to allow the President to "take care that the laws are faithfully executed" by allowing him or her control of those personnel who are charged with executing the law. The Court also rejected the narrower position that Article II vests such removal authority in the President when the officer at issue is engaged in a core executive function, such as prosecuting violations of the law. Instead, the Court stated that the rule was whether a statute's restrictions on his or her removal authority "are of such a nature that they impede the President's ability to perform his [or her] constitutional duty." In *Morrison*, the Court applied this test to uphold a statute allowing the President's agent (the Attorney General) to remove a special prosecutor only for "good cause."

Here, too, we have a good-cause removal provision. The restriction on the President's removal authority is probably constitutional under *Morrison*. If anything, the restriction here is on more solid constitutional ground since the inferior officer at issue is not one solely engaged in a core executive function like prosecuting; rather, he or she is also engaged in quasi-legislative functions (promulgating regulations) and quasi-judicial functions (adjudicating violations of the law). The Court in *Morrison* noted that this analysis of the type of functions played by the officer was not dispositive, but it was also not irrelevant. See *Morrison*, discussing and distinguishing *Humphrey's Executor v. United States*, 295 U.S. 602 (1935).

However, the congressional role in removing the officer is likely unconstitutional. In *Morrison*, the Court cautioned that, while Congress had significant latitude to restrict presidential control over appointment and removal of inferior officers, Congress could not attempt to aggrandize itself by retaining control over their appointment or removal. Here, the statute allows either the President *or Congress* to remove the officer. This aggrandizement of congressional power is probably unconstitutional under *Morrison*.

4. Administrative Adjudicatory Scheme: The final question is whether the statute violates Article III of the Constitution. Article III vests "the judicial power of the United States" in federal courts, whose judges enjoy life tenure and salary security. The ALJs here do not — they are judges for only five-year periods and are always subject to dismissal. Thus, the question is whether the statute can vest some of "the judicial power" in these non–Article III judges.

In *Commodities Futures Trading Corp. v. Schor*, 478 U.S. 833 (1986), the Court set forth a three-pronged test to judge such claims. The first prong essentially asks about the degree to which the agency court (or "Article I court") enjoys the powers of an Article III court, and, conversely, the amount of control that an Article III court retains. The criteria here include the breadth and permissive or mandatory nature of the agency court's jurisdiction, its powers, and the review authority that the Article III court has over the agency court's decisions.

Here, the agency court enjoys relatively limited jurisdiction, over claims related to statutory violations and counterclaims arising out of those same facts. The *Schor* Court looked favorably on a similar jurisdiction grant to the agency court in that case. The agency court does have the authority to enforce its own orders, which suggests a power normally associated with an Article III court. The statute suggests that the agency court's jurisdiction is permissive, rather than mandatory, which cuts in favor of the statute's constitutionality.

An important issue is the intensity of the Article III court review of the agency court's decisions. In *Schor*, the Court accepted the statute's relatively deferential Article III court review of the agency court's fact findings; however, it also noted that Article III courts reviewed the agency court's legal conclusions *de novo* (*i.e.*, without any deference at all). Here, by contrast, both the agency court's fact findings and legal conclusions are reviewed under the highly deferential "clear error" standard. The deferential review of the agency court's legal conclusions would present a significant problem, given the centrality of Article III courts' power to interpret the law. This factor would cut strongly against the statute.

A second basic *Schor* factor concerns the nature of the right being litigated. *Schor* distinguished between "private" and "public" rights. The definitions of these terms are not completely clear. However, at their most basic, private rights are rights between two private parties, based on the common law, while public rights are rights between a private party and the federal government, based on federal statutory law. Agency court adjudication of public rights has never been thought to present a problem, while in *Schor*, the fact that the agency court was litigating a private right cut against the statute's adjudication scheme.

Here, the main concern would be the agency court's litigation of counterclaims, which would not only involve two private parties but also might be based on the common law (*e.g.*, contract or tort law). This factor would cut against the constitutionality of the statute in a context where the agency court sought to take jurisdiction over a common-law counterclaim.

The final factor weighed in *Schor* was the motives Congress had for taking away power from the federal courts. In *Schor*, the Court noted that Congress wanted to set up an efficient and quick way for persons to vindicate their commodities fraud claims. It also noted that commodities futures was a highly technical area where generalist Article III judges might not have the expertise to make accurate decisions. Finally, it noted that it made sense to give the agency court jurisdiction over common-law counterclaims arising out of the commodities transactions that were the subject of the statutory violations claims, since it was more efficient and led to better results to have one court adjudicate all the claims arising out of a particular transaction. Notably, the Court did not find that Congress was simply motivated by a desire to punish Article III courts for reaching rulings that angered Congress.

Here, the statute's findings indicate a concern that the Internet is changing so rapidly that judges need to be expert in online technology. There is also no evidence that Congress sought to strip Article III courts of their jurisdiction to punish them or to force certain types of results. For this reason, this factor would probably cut, at least weakly, in favor of the statute's constitutionality.

In sum, the first factor would count against the statute's constitutionality, given the relatively small role that Article III courts play in reviewing the agency court's legal conclusions and the agency court's ability to enforce its own judgments. The second factor would cut against constitutionality as well, to the extent that it authorized the agency court to adjudicate private rights. The third factor would cut in favor of the statute.

While the *Schor* test is a vague balancing test with no combination of factors dispositive, the discretion agency courts enjoy under Factor 1 and their jurisdiction over private rights claims in Factor 2 may well lead a court to strike the statute down.

QUESTION #2

In general, when an agency interprets a statute, a court will apply either the deference level from *Chevron USA v. Natural Resources Defense Council*, 467 U.S. 837 (1984) or from *Skidmore v. Swift & Co.*, 323 U.S. 134 (1944). The rule from *United States v. Mead Corp.*, 533 U.S. 218 (2001), is that, in general, if the agency is given power to act via rulemaking, and it interprets the statute while exercising that power, then *Chevron* deference is appropriate. The basic idea underlying this general rule is that *Chevron* deference rests on the court's conclusion that Congress implicitly intended to delegate to the agency the power to act with the force of law, and that the agency utilized that delegation when it interpreted the statute (*Mead*). According to *Mead*, an important indicator of this intent is whether Congress authorized the agency to act pursuant to careful procedures (such as rulemaking and formal adjudication) that are generally considered appropriate when an agency wishes to act with the force of law — *i.e.*, such that a court would respect any reasonable interpretive choice made by the agency.

However, *Mead* also noted that sometimes the requisite congressional intent will be found even when the agency has not acted pursuant to careful procedures. See *Mead* (citing *NationsBank v. Variable Annuity Life Ins. Co.*, 513 U.S. 251 (1995) (where *Chevron* deference was given even though the agency had not acted pursuant to these procedures)). Because the agency action challenged in *Mead* did not follow these procedures, the *Mead* Court examined the details of the particular agency action for which *Chevron* deference was being requested.

In performing that examination, the *Mead* Court noted several characteristics of the challenged agency action (a decision by the U.S. Customs Service to classify a particular imported product as one type of item rather than another). It noted that the agency decision applied only to imports of identical items, that it was subject to revocation without any notice except to the person at whom the original decision was targeted, and that the decision warned third parties not to rely on it. It also noted that the decision needed only be made available for public inspection (*i.e.*, it did not have to be published). These decisions were not promulgated pursuant to a notice-and-comment process, and in most cases, they could be revoked without such a process. Finally, it noted that these decisions could be issued by any of 46 port-of-entry Customs offices and observed that approximately 10,000 to 15,000 such decisions were issued per year. Based on these factors, the *Mead* Court declined to give these rulings *Chevron* deference.

Here, the facts provided mirror closely the Customs rulings that were denied *Chevron* deference in *Mead*. While the matter is not completely free of doubt given the vagueness of the Court's implied delegation analysis, the closeness between *Mead*'s facts and the facts of this case suggest that a court in this case would not give *Chevron* deference.

In *Mead*, the Court, after rejecting *Chevron* deference, remanded the case to the lower courts so they could apply *Skidmore* deference. In *Skidmore*, the Court explained what this deference meant: "We consider [the agency's views] . . . while not controlling upon the courts by reason of their authority, do constitute a body of experience and informed judgment to which courts and litigants may properly resort for guidance. The weight of such a judgment in a particular case will depend on the thoroughness evidence in its consideration, the validity of its reasoning, its consistency with earlier and later pronouncements, and all those factors which give it power to persuade, if not lacking power to control."

How does this differ from *Chevron* deference? Under the *Chevron* test, the Court first determines whether the statute clearly answers the question at issue, using "traditional tools of statutory construction." If the court finds a clear meaning, it applies it. If the court can't, it will defer to any reasonable agency interpretation of the statute.

Essentially, then, *Skidmore* deference means deference that varies based on the persuasiveness of the agency's interpretive argument. If that argument is based on careful consideration of the issues and good reasoning, it will enjoy a higher degree of deference. Similarly, if the agency's interpretation is one that the agency has held consistently for a long time, it will enjoy more deference.

This is somewhat similar to *Chevron* deference, but with some important differences. First, *Chevron* deference does not examine the longstanding or consistent nature of the agency's interpretation. Indeed, *Chevron* has been justified in part as a way to allow a new presidential administration to alter an agency's interpretation of a statute to better fit the new administration's policy priorities. By contrast, *Skidmore* deference turns in part on whether the agency has maintained a consistent interpretive position over time.

Second, as explained in *Mead*, *Chevron* deference is grounded theoretically on the idea that Congress has delegated to the agency the power to act with the force of law — *i.e.*, to act such that a court must not substitute its own judgment as to the best reading of an ambiguous statute. See *Chevron* (reversing the lower court because that court, after finding the statute to be ambiguous on the issue before it, looked itself for the best interpretation of the statute instead of deferring to the agency's reasonable interpretive choice). As suggested by the above quote from *Skidmore*, *Skidmore* deference is instead based on the idea that an agency that has thought about an issue carefully and has come up with a consistent interpretation should enjoy deference for that interpretation, exactly because that interpretation strikes the court as a trustworthy one. This reflects a different theoretical grounding for *Skidmore* deference.

Administrative Law
Multiple Choice
100 QUESTIONS

ANSWER SHEET

Print or copy this answer sheet to all multiple choice questions.

1.	A B C D	26.	A B C D	51.	A B C D	76.	A B C D
2.	A B C D	27.	A B C D	52.	A B C D	77.	A B C D
3.	A B C D	28.	A B C D	53.	A B C D	78.	A B C D
4.	A B C D	29.	A B C D	54.	A B C D	79.	A B C D
5.	A B C D	30.	A B C D	55.	A B C D	80.	A B C D
6.	A B C D	31.	A B C D	56.	A B C D	81.	A B C D
7.	A B C D	32.	A B C D	57.	A B C D	82.	A B C D
8.	A B C D	33.	A B C D	58.	A B C D	83.	A B C D
9.	A B C D	34.	A B C D	59.	A B C D	84.	A B C D
10.	A B C D	35.	A B C D	60.	A B C D	85.	A B C D
11.	A B C D	36.	A B C D	61.	A B C D	86.	A B C D
12.	A B C D	37.	A B C D	62.	A B C D	87.	A B C D
13.	A B C D	38.	A B C D	63.	A B C D	88.	A B C D
14.	A B C D	39.	A B C D	64.	A B C D	89.	A B C D
15.	A B C D	40.	A B C D	65.	A B C D	90.	A B C D
16.	A B C D	41.	A B C D	66.	A B C D	91.	A B C D
17.	A B C D	42.	A B C D	67.	A B C D	92.	A B C D
18.	A B C D	43.	A B C D	68.	A B C D	93.	A B C D
19.	A B C D	44.	A B C D	69.	A B C D	94.	A B C D
20.	A B C D	45.	A B C D	70.	A B C D	95.	A B C D
21.	A B C D	46.	A B C D	71.	A B C D	96.	A B C D
22.	A B C D	47.	A B C D	72.	A B C D	97.	A B C D
23.	A B C D	48.	A B C D	73.	A B C D	98.	A B C D
24.	A B C D	49.	A B C D	74.	A B C D	99.	A B C D
25.	A B C D	50.	A B C D	75.	A B C D	100.	A B C D

ADMINISTRATIVE LAW QUESTIONS

Questions 1–14 refer to the following item reported by the Washington Daily Tattler.
Read the item before continuing.

WASHINGTON — You know those dirty, noisy, and dangerous jet skis you see in lakes across the country? Not for much longer. The National Park Service wants to ban personal watercraft such as jet skis from most of the waterways it manages, saying they are dirty, noisy, and dangerous. The Park Service would ban them from all national parks, including nine where they are now allowed, under rules the agency has proposed. . . .

"Our mandate is to protect these places and allow visitors to use them, to ensure that they will remain pristine for future generations," Park Service spokeswoman Elaine June said Tuesday. . . .

Park Service officials plan to publish [the proposed regulations] this winter and then take public comment for 90 days, after which time the rules may be revised. They are not expected to take effect for up to a year.

"We've still got quite a ways to go," said Dennis Burnett, the Park Service's regulations manager. "This list could obviously change based on the number and type of comments we receive."

Personal watercraft makers have opposed the ban as unfair and unnecessary, arguing that new models are quieter and cleaner. Their users are becoming more courteous and safer, they say. . . .

In proposing its ban, the Park Service said personal watercraft are "often operated in an aggressive manner" and are the subject of frequent complaints about noise and unsafe operation. In addition, leaking oil and gas can foul the water. . . .

Conservationists had feared the Park Service would give local superintendents wide authority to exempt their units from the ban.

"We're delighted," said Mark Thomas, a spokesman for the National Parks and Conservation Association.

Assume that the Park Service is acting pursuant to its authority in the National Parks Administration Act. That statute reads as follows:

§1: The Congress hereby finds that National Parks are a vital resource to Americans seeking recreational activities of all types, and play a crucial role in ensuring the continued existence of wild, pristine, and unspoiled areas for future generations and the continued existence of endangered plant and animal species.

§2: The National Park Service shall ensure, to the extent feasible, that National Parks provide recreational facilities for Americans of all interests and hobbies, consistent with protection of the natural environment and endangered species that may live in such parks.

§3: The Park Service shall have the authority to promulgate, after hearing, regulations to carry out its statutory mandate.

§4: Within 5 days of promulgating a regulation pursuant to §3, the Park Service shall forward a copy of such regulation to the House Committee on the Interior, and the Senate Sub-Committee on National Parks. Such regulation shall not take effect for 60 days after transmittal to both committees. During this 60-day period, Congress may prevent any such regulation from taking effect if a majority of each house approves a joint resolution expressing disapproval.

1. Is §4 constitutional?

A) Yes.

B) No: The problem is that Congress cannot delay the effective date of a regulation otherwise validly promulgated.

C) No: There is no problem with the 60-day waiting period, but there is a problem with referring validly promulgated regulations for legislative review.

D) No: There is no problem with the 60-day waiting period or the referral requirement, but there is a problem with the legislative disapproval provision.

2. Which of the following statements most accurately reflects the probable judicial response to a claim that the statute unconstitutionally delegates legislative power to the agency?

A) The statute might well be struck down because it reflects Congress's failure to make a clear value choice between environmental protection and accommodation of all recreational interests in the national parks.

B) The statute would probably not be struck down: Courts routinely uphold broad, nearly standardless delegations of power to agencies.

C) The statute would probably not be struck down: The only statutes ever struck down on nondelegation grounds have involved delegation of adjudicatory, not legislative, power.

D) The statute would probably not be struck down because it requires the agency simply to make factual determinations about the best accommodation of recreational and conservation interests.

3. Which of the following statements most accurately reflects the procedure that the agency would have to follow in promulgating the jet ski rule?

A) The agency would have to provide whatever hearing would be appropriate under the *Mathews v. Eldridge* due process analysis.

B) The agency would have to provide a hearing of the sort contemplated by the APA's notice-and-comment procedures.

C) The agency would have to provide an oral hearing, with the right to cross-examine witnesses.

D) The agency would not have to follow any particular procedure unless a court decided that the importance of the issue justified a particular level of procedural formality.

4. Assume for purposes of this question that the National Parks Act explicitly specifies that the agency should follow the APA's notice-and-comment procedures when promulgating rules. Which of the following statements about those procedures is most accurate?

   I. The agency would be required to disclose the most important data that it has about the number of accidents involving jet skis in national parks and about jet skis' contribution to water pollution in national parks.

   II. The agency might be required to employ procedures more formal than those set forth in the notice-and-comment rules if a court determined that the social importance of the issue justified more formal procedures.

   III. If the agency had to modify its proposed list of banned watercraft significantly based on the comments that it received from the public, it might be required to conduct a second round of notice-and-comment procedures on its modified rule.

   IV. The agency might be required to supplement the notice-and-comment procedures with whatever extra procedures might be required by the Due Process Clause.

   A) I only.

   B) I, II, and III only.

   C) I and III only.

   D) III and IV only.

5. Assume for the purpose of this question that the agency embarks on a formal rulemaking process of the sort specified in the APA. During the oral hearing, an agency expert testifies on the environmental degradation caused by the use of jet skis in national parks. After the hearing is over, the agency official that presided at the hearing decides that he needs more information about the toxicity of jet ski fuel. How could the hearing officer go about getting that information from the expert?

   A) The hearing officer could call the expert on the telephone and ask the question.

   B) The hearing officer would have to reopen the hearing so that all parties could be present when the expert answers the question.

C) B is the correct answer, with the caveat that if the matter were on appeal to the head of the agency, the agency head could telephone the expert and ask the question.

D) The hearing officer could telephone the expert and ask the question, but he would have to record the substance of the conversation in a memo that would be placed in the case file for public inspection.

6. Assume for the purpose of this question that, before beginning any rulemaking, the head of the National Park Service gives a well-publicized speech before the Sierra Club in which he criticizes use of off-road motorcycles and jet skis in national parks, stating "surely, serving the legitimate recreational needs of Americans does not require us to admit into our parks limitless numbers of smoke-belching, noisy, dangerous contraptions whose very presence is an affront to the basic purpose of our park system." What effect would this speech have on the agency's ability to commence a rulemaking on the subject of whether the use of jet skis in national parks should be limited?

A) The agency head would probably have to recuse himself from any participation in the rulemaking to ensure the appearance of fairness that is fundamental to public confidence in the administrative process.

B) The agency head would probably have to recuse himself from any participation in the rulemaking process only if it were shown that he had an unalterably closed mind on this issue.

C) The agency head would not have to recuse himself, so long as the subject of the rulemaking was changed from *whether* there should be limits on jet skis in parks, to *what sort* of limits there should be; this change would reflect the fact that the agency already has taken a position that some limits on jet skis are appropriate.

D) The agency head would not have to recuse himself.

7. Assume for the purpose of this question that agency publishes the following notice in the *Federal Register*:

> "Today, the National Park Service announces adoption of a general policy that jet skis should be banned from national parks between Memorial Day and Labor Day. This policy will guide the agency in making determinations about use of jet skis in particular parks during particular months. Due to its status as a policy statement, this statement will not be subject to a notice-and-comment rulemaking process."

Which of the following statements is most accurate?

A) The agency would probably be forced to conduct a notice-and-comment procedure: General statements of policy are not exempt from the notice-and-comment process.

B) The agency would probably be forced to conduct a notice-and-comment procedure: General statements of policy are exempt from the notice-and-comment process, but courts almost never accept agency claims that one of its pronouncements is in fact merely a policy statement.

C) If the agency was successful in asserting that this was a general statement of policy, the agency would not have to go through the notice-and-comment process, but it would have to litigate the wisdom of the prohibition policy in every enforcement action.

D) The agency would probably **NOT** be forced to conduct a notice-and-comment procedure: General statements of policy are nowhere mentioned in the section of the APA setting forth the notice-and-comment procedures, and thus they are presumed to be exempt from those procedures.

Assume for the purpose of the rest of the jet ski questions (Questions 8–14) that the agency promulgates a final regulation banning jet skis from national parks between Memorial Day and Labor Day.

8. Jet Skiers International, an association of jet ski enthusiasts, wishes to challenge the regulation immediately. Which of the following statements most accurately describes the availability of such immediate, pre-enforcement review?

   A) Such review would never be available because it could never be a case or controversy.

   B) Such review would be available only if the National Park Act explicitly authorized it; if the statute does not contain this authority, review could take place only in the course of the agency's attempt to enforce the ban.

   C) Such review would generally be available unless Congress manifested a clear intent to preclude it, but such review could still be blocked if a court determined that the issue would be better illuminated by the facts of an actual enforcement action.

   D) Such review would always be available if a court determined that the private party would suffer significant hardship if forced to wait for an actual enforcement action.

9. Which of the following statements most accurately describes the law governing the standing of a group like Jet Skiers International to sue in Question 8?

   A) It could sue only if a citizen-suit provision authorized such a lawsuit.

   B) It could sue only if one of its members had standing, unless Congress abrogated this requirement.

   C) It could sue only if the relief that it sought would be effective in the absence of any individual member of the association as a named plaintiff, unless Congress abrogated this requirement.

D) The only restrictions on associations suing are those found in Article III's case or controversy requirement; the zone of interests test sweeps all other prudential barriers aside.

10. Assume that WaveRider, a major manufacturer of jet skis, wishes to challenge the agency's regulation. Which of the following statements most accurately describes the APA provision governing its standing to sue?

A) As only an indirect victim of the jet ski ban, it would not have standing.

B) The APA's standing provision explicitly removes all prudential barriers to standing, leaving only the restrictions of Article III's case or controversy requirement.

C) WaveRider would have to satisfy the zone of interests test; this would require examination of whether producers of recreational boating equipment actively lobbied Congress during its deliberations on the National Parks Act.

D) WaveRider would have to satisfy the zone of interests test; this would require only that its interests be arguably within the zone of interests sought to be protected by the statute.

11. In drafting a complaint seeking judicial review of the regulation, which of the following could WaveRider cite as the basis for the federal court's jurisdiction?

   I. APA Section 704

   II. The general federal question jurisdiction statute (28 U.S.C. §1331)

   III. The doctrine of pendent federal jurisdiction

     A) I and II only.

     B) I, II, and III.

     C) II only.

     D) I only.

12. Assume that WaveRider sues the agency, arguing that the jet ski ban reflects a misreading of the statute. Which of the following statements most accurately describes how the court would analyze the issue?

A) The court would first examine whether the text of the statute clearly answered the question; if it did not, the court would not look at legislative history or any other interpretive clue but instead would simply defer to any reasonable agency interpretation.

B) The court would first examine whether the statute clearly answered the question, using any and all traditional tools of statutory interpretation; the court would defer to the agency's interpretation only if that examination failed to yield a clear answer.

C) Since this is an issue of statutory interpretation, the court would not defer to the agency's interpretation but would reach its own independent conclusion as to the statute's meaning.

D) Normally, a court would defer to any reasonable agency interpretation, but not in this case; since the agency's interpretation was announced in a regulation (as opposed to an adjudication), a court would probably consider this a pure question of statutory interpretation and reach its own independent conclusion as to the statute's meaning.

13. Assume for the purpose of this question that the agency promulgates its jet ski rule after following the APA's notice-and-comment procedures. In its lawsuit, WaveRider argues that the agency made serious errors of logic and analysis when it determined that the jet ski ban was an appropriate response to the problem at hand, and thus it claims that the ban was arbitrary and capricious. Which of the following statement(s) is/are accurate?

I. The arbitrary and capricious standard is essentially the same as the rational basis standard in constitutional law; thus, if the court is able to hypothesize a reasonable explanation for the agency's action, it will uphold that action.

II. The arbitrary and capricious standard essentially asks whether the agency considered all the relevant factors and whether the agency committed a clear error of judgment.

III. The arbitrary and capricious standard requires that the agency's decision be supportable solely on the basis of the public rulemaking record; thus, the court would reject any attempt by the agency to rely on internal agency analysis as support for the jet ski ban.

IV. The arbitrary and capricious standard would not apply since the agency had engaged in notice-and-comment rulemaking.

A) II and III only.

B) III only.

C) II only.

D) I, II, and IV only.

14. Assume for the purpose of this question that the agency promulgates its jet ski rule after following the APA's notice-and-comment procedures. WaveRider's challenge includes a claim that during the rulemaking process, the Sierra Club provided to the Office of Management and Budget (OMB) technical data about jet skis' contribution to water pollution in national parks, and that OMB in turn passed this information on to the Park Service. Assume further that the Park Service is part of the Department of the Interior, which is an

executive-branch agency (*i.e.*, it is not independent). What would be the result, under the executive orders on regulatory oversight that have been in effect since the early 1990s?

A) The court would strike the rule down on that ground, since those orders prohibit this sort of funneling.

B) The court would not strike the rule down on that ground; this type of *ex parte* contact is not prohibited in rulemaking.

C) The court would probably not strike the rule down on that ground; this may be a violation of the APA but such procedural violations are subject to a harmless error rule.

D) The court would probably not strike the rule down on that ground; these orders make clear that violations do not give private parties any extra rights enforceable by a court against an agency.

Questions 15–16 refer to the following situation.

Sam Louis is an Army veteran who until recently received veterans disability benefits from the government based on a hearing loss that he suffered during combat in the Gulf War of 1991. One month ago, he received a letter from the government informing him that his next monthly check would be his last, as the government had reviewed his file and concluded that he was no longer eligible for disability benefits. The disability statute states that the only recourse for claimants alleging wrongful denial of benefits is an oral hearing held within three months after the benefit cutoff.

15. Which of the following, if true, would be most helpful to Sam's claim that his right to veterans benefits is a property interest protected by the Due Process Clause?

A) Sam needs the benefits to live, as he has no other source of income.

B) The Veterans Administration (VA) regulations, which Sam has never read, provide that hearing loss constitutes a disability and that disabled veterans are eligible for benefits.

C) The VA did not provide an attorney or non-attorney legal advocate for any claimant who desired one.

D) Congress, in enacting the disability statute, recognized that many disabled veterans are unable to work.

16. Assuming that a court determined that Sam had a due process property interest in his benefits, which of the following best describes the analysis that the court would probably use in determining whether the statute complied with the Due Process Clause?

A) Since all property stands on equal footing before the Constitution, once the court determined that Sam had a property interest, it would probably require the agency to provide pre-deprivation trial-type procedures before it could deprive him of his benefits.

B) Since Sam's expectation of benefits was explicitly conditioned by the procedure that Congress provided for challenging benefit cutoff decisions, the court would probably hold that Sam was due only the procedure that the statute in fact provided.

C) The court would probably balance several factors, including the extra accuracy that might be expected from additional procedures, and the general importance of these benefits to the recipients.

D) Since these benefits are provided as a matter of legislative grace, the court would probably require less procedure here than in the case of government action threatening a traditional common-law property right.

17. Which of the following statements about due process is most accurate?

A) The doctrine of "the bitter with the sweet," which is part of modern due process doctrine, limits the coverage of the Due Process Clause by looking to the procedural protections attached to the statutory grant of "new property" benefits.

B) Due process aims primarily at ensuring that individuals deprived of valuable interests feel that they have had a fair procedure, thus making the deprivation seem more legitimate.

C) The due process inquiry is a unitary one, *i.e.*, all the relevant questions are answered in a single balancing test.

D) The doctrine of "new property" has significantly increased the types of interests protected by due process.

Questions 18–20 deal with the following situation.

In 1999, Congress enacts "the Securities Investors' Protection Act of 1999" (SIPA). The statute reads as follows:

§1: *Findings:* Congress hereby finds:
1. that increased public participation in the stock market provides vast public benefits, including reduction in the need for public financing of retirement programs; but
2. that this increased public participation is placed at risk by stockbrokers' use of contracts that are decipherable only by sophisticated investors; and
3. that increased public confidence in their stock brokers, by use of easy to understand contractual language, will benefit all parties to the transaction, including brokers, who will reap the benefits of increased public willingness to invest in stocks.

§2: *Use of Clear Language:* Any stock broker whose conduct substantially affects interstate commerce shall use contracts that feature contractual language appropriate to the degree of sophistication of the customer, taking into account the complexity and size of the transaction.

§3: *Rulemaking Authority:* The Securities and Exchange Commission (SEC) is hereby authorized to promulgate rules enforcing the requirements of §2.

§4: *Fines:* Any violation of this statute or any regulation promulgated pursuant to §3 shall be punished by a fine not to exceed $10,000 per occurrence.

§5: *Enforcement Authority:* The SEC may enforce this statute, and any regulations promulgated pursuant to §3, by bringing a civil suit in any federal district court in which venue is proper.

18. Six months after this statute is enacted, the SEC brings an enforcement action against Smith Securities ("Smith"), alleging that its standard-form stock options contract violates §2 and seeking a fine of $200 million, on the ground that in the prior six months, the firm had entered into 20,000 options contracts with customers (20,000 occurrences × $10,000 per occurrence = $200 million). Smith objects that the agency abused its discretion by bringing a lawsuit against it, as opposed to promulgating a regulation that would apply to all stockbrokers. Which of the following results would best reflect the current state of Supreme Court jurisprudence on this question?

   A) The court would probably reject Smith's claim, on the ground that absent specific statutory direction to use one or another means, agencies retain absolute discretion to proceed by adjudication or rulemaking or any combination thereof.

   B) The court would probably reject Smith's claim, on the ground that absent specific statutory direction to use one or another means, agencies retain a great deal of discretion to proceed by adjudication or rulemaking or any combination thereof.

   C) The court would probably reject Smith's claim unless there was a pending rulemaking on this same topic, in which case fundamental fairness would require that Smith not be singled out through an enforcement action.

   D) The court would probably reject Smith's claim unless Smith could show that the disputed issues in the enforcement action concerned legislative facts that would be more effectively resolved in a rulemaking process.

19. Assume that a major financial scandal erupts when it is disclosed that a large discount brokerage firm has been using technical contractual language to cheat investors out of large sums of money. A group formed to protect investors' rights sues the SEC, claiming that its refusal to bring an enforcement action against the broker represents an abuse of discretion. What would be the result?

   A) The court would probably not reach the merits of the claim on the grounds that the agency conduct was unreviewable.

B) The court would probably reach the merits of the claim but then reject it, given the broad deference customarily accorded agency decisions not to prosecute.

C) The court would probably reach the merits of the claim, and might well find for the plaintiffs, given the sometimes-strict interpretation of the arbitrary and capricious standard.

D) The court would probably not reach the merits of the claim on the ground that the plaintiffs failed the zone of interests test.

20. After the SEC promulgates strict regulations restricting brokers and begins aggressive enforcement of those regulations, in 2011 the President attempts to remove the head of the SEC for following policies inconsistent with the President's pro-deregulation philosophy. Upon being barred from his office and deprived of his salary, the head of the SEC brings a lawsuit for back pay and restoration of his office. The Securities Exchange Act of 1934 specifies that the head of the SEC shall serve one seven-year term and be removable only for "good cause." He was appointed in 1998. What result?

A) The President wins: Officials charged with administering the laws (such as SIPA) must be removable at the President's will to protect the President's constitutional power to execute the laws.

B) The SEC head wins: Congress has complete authority to immunize agency heads from removal at will.

C) The SEC head wins: Congress may immunize an agency head from presidential removal power so long as Congress, as the other politically accountable branch, retains its own power to remove the agency head.

D) The SEC head wins: Congress may immunize an agency head from removal at will if it has a good reason for doing so and if doing so will not unduly impair the President's constitutional responsibility for executing the laws.

Questions 21–29 refer to the following statute.

In response to a serious aviation accident, Congress enacts a statute regulating the transport of flammable cargo on passenger airlines. The statute reads as follows:

§1: The Congress hereby finds that the carriage of flammable materials on board commercial aircraft, while sometimes necessary for interstate commerce and the financial viability of airlines, nevertheless poses a significant safety risk to the traveling public. Public perception of this risk discourages passenger air travel.

§2: No commercial air flight originating or terminating in the United States shall carry cargo which the Secretary of Transportation deems "extremely flammable" or "flammable."

§3: No commercial air flight originating or terminating in the United States shall carry cargo which the Secretary of Transportation deems "potentially flammable" unless such cargo is carried in such a manner as to minimize, to the extent feasible, the possibility of accidental combustion, taking into account the costs of providing safeguards against such combustion.

§4: Within 180 days of the enactment of this statute, the Secretary of Transportation shall, after hearing, promulgate regulations implementing the requirements of this statute.

§5: Regulations promulgated pursuant to §4 shall not take effect for 60 days. During this 60-day period, Congress may prevent any such regulation from taking effect if a majority of both houses express disapproval.

§6: Violations of this statute, or any regulations validly promulgated pursuant to this statute, may be punished by a fine of up to $50,000 per occurrence. The DOT may bring charges that a person has violated such regulations. Such charges shall be decided by a DOT Administrative Law Judge (ALJ), on the record after opportunity for agency hearing, with a right of appeal to the Secretary of Transportation. Appeals from the Secretary's decision may be brought to the United States Court of Appeals for the D.C. Circuit, which shall review agency legal conclusions *de novo* and agency fact findings for clear error.

21. When the Department of Transportation fails to bring an enforcement action against World Wide Airlines, even though press reports make it clear that World Wide habitually carries flammable materials on commercial flights, the American Federation of Travel Agents files a lawsuit seeking to compel the agency to bring such an action. What is the most likely result of this lawsuit?

    A) Even if the federation could show that its members suffered injury as a result of the agency's failure to act, a court would still probably deny the federation's standing to sue.

    B) The court would probably hold that the agency's failure to act was not reviewable by a court, given the difficult questions of resource allocation underlying decisions to prosecute.

    C) Without an explicit grant of jurisdiction in the statute, the court would probably hold that it did not have subject-matter jurisdiction to consider the claim.

    D) The court would probably reach the merits of the federation's claim.

22. Assume now that the Department of Transportation commences a rulemaking procedure to identify "flammable" and "potentially flammable" items. Which of the following statements is most accurate?

    A) The Due Process Clause of the Constitution would require that the rulemaking procedure include an opportunity for oral presentation and cross-examination.

B) The Due Process Clause would not require that the rulemaking procedure include an opportunity for oral presentation and cross-examination, but the APA would.

C) Neither the Due Process Clause nor the APA would require that the rulemaking procedure include an opportunity for oral presentation and cross-examination.

D) Under the "hard look" doctrine, a court might require that the rulemaking procedure include an opportunity for oral presentation and cross-examination, depending on the court's estimation of the social importance of the issue that was the subject of the rulemaking.

23. Assume now that as a result of the rulemaking procedure, the agency classifies as "flammable" two substances, crylon and zorac, that by themselves are completely harmless, but that can cause a fire when their fumes intermingle. Crow Chemical, which manufactures crylon, sues the agency, claiming that Congress did not intend to restrict the transportation of substances such as these, that were in themselves nonflammable. Which of the following would best describe the result of the court's standing analysis?

A) Crow would have standing: All that is required for standing is injury; since Crow would be injured by the rule, it would have standing to sue.

B) Crow would have standing: In addition to injury, a plaintiff must be within the zone of interests sought to be protected by the statute; here, the congressional finding suggests a concern with interstate shipment of goods, thus placing a manufacturer of such goods within the statute's zone of interests.

C) Crow would not have standing: The restriction on shipment of such goods indicates that crylon manufacturers would not have a legal right under the statute and thus would not have standing to sue.

D) Crow would not have standing: In addition to injury, a plaintiff must be within the zone of interests sought to be protected by the statute; this is a stringent test that in this case would probably be met only by an airline itself or by a group representing passengers.

24. Assume that National Airlines sues the agency, making the same claim Crow made in Question 23. Assuming that National has standing, which of the following statements is most accurate?

A) Since the agency is construing the statute on a topic where the statute itself does not directly answer the question, the court would probably defer to the agency's interpretation so long as it was a reasonable reading of the statute.

B) Since the promulgation of a regulation involves a pure question of law, due process would require that the court interpret the statute without regard to the agency's own interpretation.

C) Since the statute did not directly answer the question, the court would hold that the issue was committed to the agency's discretion by law, and thus it is unreviewable by a court.

D) Since the statute did not directly answer the question, the court would hold the statute invalid as a violation of the nondelegation doctrine.

25. Is §5 of the statute constitutional?

A) Yes.

B) No: The problem with §5 is that Congress cannot delay the effective date of a regulation that otherwise was validly promulgated.

C) No: There is no problem with the 60-day waiting period, but there is a problem with the legislative disapproval provision.

D) No: Congress can neither impose the 60-day waiting period nor include this sort of legislative disapproval provision.

26. Which of the following statements best describes the law governing the type of deference that a court would give to the agency's interpretation of the statute included within a regulation promulgated by the agency?

A) The fact that the agency used a rulemaking process to interpret the statute means that the interpretation will probably receive *Skidmore* deference.

B) The fact that the agency used a rulemaking process to interpret the statute means that the interpretation will probably receive *Chevron* deference.

C) The fact that the agency used a rulemaking process to interpret the statute would be irrelevant to the type of deference the interpretation received.

D) The fact that the agency used a rulemaking process to interpret the statute would be relevant only if the agency used formal rulemaking, given the increased protections for participation rights implied by formal rulemaking processes.

27. The Department of Transportation (DOT) charges Clear Skies Airlines with violating the statute by carrying a substance deemed "flammable." Clear Skies brings a suit in federal court requesting a declaratory judgment that the statute's ALJ adjudication provisions are unconstitutional. Which of the following statements are accurate?

I. The only arguable claim that Clear Skies could make would be based on the separation of powers.

II. Clear Skies could make arguable claims based both on separation of powers and due process.

III. The standards of review set forth in the statute suggest that the statute will be found constitutional.

IV. The nature of the issue being litigated—*i.e.*, whether it is a public or a private right—suggests that the statute will be found unconstitutional.

V. The nature of the issue being litigated—*i.e.*, whether it is a public or a private right—will be irrelevant to the court's analysis of the statute's constitutionality.

A) I and III only.

B) II and IV only.

C) II and III only.

D) III and V only.

28. Assume that Clear Skies does not challenge the constitutionality of the ALJ adjudication provisions but chooses instead to defend itself before the ALJ. The agency charges that Clear Skies transported a load of brass polish. The agency's regulations do not mention brass polish as "flammable," but the agency's position is that brass polish is a "caustic chemical," which the regulations do in fact classify as "flammable." After oral argument, the ALJ wishes to speak with a DOT expert (who was not otherwise connected with the investigation) to ask her whether, in her opinion, brass polish is a "caustic chemical." Which of the following best describes the law governing the permissibility of that question?

A) It is clear that the ALJ could ask the question in whatever setting he chose.

B) The ALJ could ask the question only if he did so outside the presence of both sides' attorneys.

C) The ALJ could ask the agency's attorney to ask the expert and to submit the response in a confidential submission filed only with the ALJ.

D) The ALJ could ask the question if he gave notice to both sides and gave both sides a chance to cross-examine the expert.

29. On appeal to the Secretary of Transportation, could the Secretary ask the question referenced in Question 28?

A) Yes: but only on notice and opportunity for all parties to participate in the questioning.

B) Yes: The agency head could ask the question, even without giving notice to the parties.

C) Yes: The agency head could ask the question with the same restrictions as would apply to the ALJ.

D) No: The agency head could not ask the question; the information could be obtained only if an attorney for one of the parties called the expert as a witness and questioned her.

Questions 30–33 refer to the following news article.

Protests Mean Delay on Organic Food Rules
By *The Minneapolis World*

WASHINGTON—Amid big protests from farmers and organics interest groups, Agriculture Secretary Roger Smith said today that he would put off action on new national labeling rules for organic food for 60 days to allow for more public comment.

The Agriculture Department has already received more than 2,500 comments on the proposed rules, many objecting to their alleged leniency in allowing foods to be labeled "organic." The statute requires the agency to use what in administrative law is known as "notice-and-comment" rulemaking.

But Mr. Smith noted that the department had taken no stand on those issues and wanted to hear from the public about them.

"This rule is not the last word and does not reflect how U.S.D.A. will finally resolve the many difficult issues involved," Mr. Smith said.

The rules stemmed from a recent law intended to provide a national definition and label requirements for organic food. But many organic producers say the national rules will be weaker. . . .

Mr. Smith has scheduled public hearings in Texas, New Hampshire, Iowa, and Georgia on the organics rules and is encouraging people to forward comments through the Internet.

30. Which of the following statements is most accurate?

A) The APA would not require the hearings noted in the article; however, if the department did decide to hold such hearings, due process would require that their format satisfy the requirements of *Mathews v. Eldridge*.

B) The APA would not require the hearings noted in the article unless the authorizing statute required that the agency act only "on the record after opportunity for an agency hearing."

C) The APA would require oral hearings unless the department found that written submissions would be an adequate substitute.

D) The APA would not require the hearings noted in the article unless the statute provided that the rules be promulgated "after hearing."

31. Assume that during the rulemaking process, BigAg, a major agribusiness conglomerate, held meetings with the Director of the OMB and submitted technical information addressing the types of additives that render a crop inorganic. Which of the following statements best describes what OMB can or must do with that information?

    A) OMB must disclose the information to the public by maintaining a log that is open to public review.

    B) OMB is authorized to, but need not, disclose the information to the public by maintaining a log that is open to public review.

    C) OMB must disclose the information only to the agency responsible for promulgating the regulation — here, the Agriculture Department.

    D) OMB has no authority to disclose the information to any other individual or agency.

32. Which of the following statements about extensions of rulemaking comment periods is most accurate?

    A) The extension of such periods is completely within the discretion of the agency.

    B) The APA explicitly provides that comment periods shall be extended "when a fair rulemaking process" so requires.

    C) Judicial interpretations of the APA require extensions of comment periods when subsequent information leads the agency to a conclusion that is no longer the logical outgrowth of its previously proposed rule.

    D) Answer choice **C** states the correct law before *Vermont Yankee Nuclear Power Corp. v. Natural Resources Defense Council*, 435 U.S. 519 (1978); after that case, though, such liberal readings of the APA are of questionable validity.

33. Which of the following statements most accurately reflects the review that a court would probably give to the final regulation promulgated by the Agriculture Department?

    A) The review would be limited to the process by which the agency acted; any substantive review would be nothing more than a *pro-forma* review similar to the rational basis standard in constitutional law.

    B) The review would be wide-ranging, including both a potentially searching "hard look" review under the "arbitrary and capricious" standard and a careful review of the agency's rulemaking procedure, with the possibility that the court would require more procedures based on its estimate of the importance of the subject matter of the regulation.

    C) The court's substantive review of the regulation would be based solely on the information disclosed to the public during the rulemaking process.

D) The review would include a potentially searching substantive review under the arbitrary and capricious standard and a careful review, based on the requirements of §553, of the agency's rulemaking procedure.

34. Which of the following statements about associational standing is/are true?

  I. For an association to sue, it must show that the requested judicial relief would be effective in the absence of the member on whose behalf the association was suing. Congress may not abrogate this requirement.

  II. Associations may sue only when their members would not themselves have standing to sue.

  III. Normally, associations may not seek injunctive relief.

  IV. Congress may determine that a particular type of judicial relief would be effective in the absence of the member on whose behalf the association was suing.

  A) I only.

  B) IV only.

  C) I and II only.

  D) III and IV only.

35. After turning over information about its operations to a federal government agency, your client finds out that a competitor is seeking that information by making a request under the Freedom of Information Act (FOIA). Which of the following accurately states the law about arguments that you could make to prevent the agency from disclosing the information?

  I. No steps would be successful: Such "reverse FOIA" claims have been rejected by the courts.

  II. If the information fell within one of FOIA's exceptions, the agency would be legally required to refuse the competitor's request.

  III. If the information fell within one of FOIA's exceptions, the agency might be acting arbitrarily and capriciously in disclosing the information.

  IV. Only information actually generated by the government itself falls under FOIA's mandate; thus, it would be a legal error for the agency to disclose your client's information.

  V. All information in the government's possession falls within FOIA's mandate; however, information generated by the government itself is subject to mandatory disclosure, while information merely obtained by the government from private parties is subject to agency discretion to withhold.

  A) I only.

  B) III only.

C) III and V only.

D) II and IV only.

36. Frank Thompson owns a gun shop. One day, he is surprised when officials of the federal office of Alcohol, Tobacco, and Firearms show up to inspect his records. The officials do not have a warrant. Can they enter and conduct their inspection without Frank's consent?

A) No: The Fourth Amendment requires a warrant, and in the absence of the type of exigent circumstances normally associated with the Fourth Amendment, they cannot search without a warrant.

B) No: The Fourth Amendment does not itself apply to administrative searches, but the Supreme Court has read the APA to impose a similar requirement that would apply here.

C) Yes: A gun shop would probably be the type of closely regulated business for which the Supreme Court has made an exception to the warrant requirement.

D) Yes: The Fourth Amendment's warrant requirement does not apply to administrative officials, and there is no other law limiting administrative searches.

Questions 37–48 relate to the following hypothetical.

Last year, the imminent collapse of a major bank led the President to propose, and Congress to enact, the following statute regulating mortgage lending practices.

§1: *Definitions*

. . .

(9): "Subprime home mortgage lending" means lending under such terms and conditions that do not satisfy the home loan underwriting standards established by the United States Federal Reserve.

§2: *No Subprime Home Mortgage Lending*

It is a violation of federal law for any financial institution to engage in subprime home mortgage lending.

§3: *Standards and Regulations*

(a) The United States Federal Reserve Board shall promulgate home loan underwriting standards. Such standards shall ensure that inappropriately risky loans are not undertaken by borrowers, taking into account borrower resources, repayment history, and overall economic conditions.

(b) The United States Federal Reserve Board shall promulgate regulations to implement Section 2.

(c) Such standards and regulations shall be promulgated on the record after opportunity for agency hearing.

§4: *Violations*

Violations of this statute or any regulation or standard promulgated thereunder may be punishable by a fine of up to $1,000,000 per occurrence.

§5: *Adjudication of Violations*

(a) Agency Adjudications

Violations of this statute or of regulations or standards promulgated thereunder shall be prosecuted by the Office of Prosecutions within the Mortgage Lending Office of the Federal Reserve Board (MLO), and adjudicated by Administrative Law Judges (ALJs) within the MLO, on the record after opportunity for agency hearing. Such ALJs shall be selected by the Board of Governors of the Federal Reserve Board [*i.e.*, the agency heads]. The Board of Governors may, at their discretion, hear appeals from ALJ decisions.

(b) Federal Court Appeals

Appeals of any ALJ or Board of Governors decision may be brought in any federal district court where venue is proper. The federal district court shall review factual findings for clear error and legal conclusions *de novo*. Judgments entered into by any ALJ or the Board may be enforced only through an application to a federal court where venue is proper.

37. The MLO brings a prosecution against American Home Lending, alleging that American Home engaged in subprime home lending. American Home immediately sues in federal court, alleging that the ALJ adjudication scheme is unconstitutional. Which of the following statements about that claim is/are correct?

   I. The standards of review that the statute prescribes for federal courts in Section 5(b) are irrelevant to the constitutionality of the agency adjudication scheme.

   II. The fact that under the statute judgments can be enforced only by federal courts cuts in favor of the statute's constitutionality.

   III. The nature of the right at issue as public or private used to be crucial to the constitutionality of statutes such as this, but it is now irrelevant.

   IV. The availability of appeal to the agency heads cuts in favor of the statute's constitutionality.

   A) II and III only.

   B) II, III, and IV only.

   C) I only.

   D) II only.

38. Assume that the court rejects American Home's constitutional claim and the agency adjudication continues. During the ALJ's initial adjudication of the

claim, she decides that she needs to clarify the meaning of one of the agency's regulations by consulting with agency personnel who drafted it. Can she do so?

A) Yes, but only if the person she consults is not otherwise involved in the American Home litigation as a prosecutor or a witness.

B) Yes, but only if she gives notice to both sides and conducts the discussion as part of an on-the-record hearing.

C) Yes, with no restrictions.

D) No, as this would violate the APA.

39. Assume that the ALJ adjudicates the claim and finds against American Home. Can American Home immediately appeal the result to a federal court, or must it exhaust its administrative remedies first?

A) No: Exhaustion is an Article III requirement that courts enforce rigorously; thus, American Home must appeal to the agency head first.

B) No: Exhaustion is not an Article III requirement, but courts still rigorously enforce it; thus, American Home must appeal to the agency head first.

C) Yes: The Supreme Court has interpreted Article III to require federal courts to take jurisdiction over appeals from ALJs without waiting for the result of any internal agency appeals process.

D) It depends on whether a court would find applicable one of the several exceptions to the normal exhaustion requirement.

40. Assume that instead of prosecuting American Home, the agency does nothing, declining a citizen group's request that the agency investigate and consider prosecuting that company. Can the group challenge in court the agency's refusal?

A) No: Such decisions are presumptively unreviewable.

B) Yes: But the court will review such refusals very deferentially.

C) Yes: And the court's review of the agency's refusal may be intensive, requiring the agency to provide a reasoned explanation for its failure to prosecute.

D) No: Article II prohibits courts from ever reviewing such decisions since they are committed to the President based on his Article II power to execute the law.

41. What process must the agency use to promulgate regulations and standards under this statute?

A) Only the process required by the Due Process Clause.

B) Only the process required by the notice-and-comment provisions of the APA.

C) Only the process required by the formal rulemaking provisions of the APA.

D) Only the process required by the notice-and-comment provisions of the APA, supplemented by whatever procedures a reviewing court might think appropriate in light of the importance of the particular issue that is the subject of the rulemaking.

42. Assume for the purpose of this question that the agency heads are appointed by the President for seven-year terms and removable only by Congress and only for good cause. American Home alleges that this structure violates the Constitution. Is it a violation?

A) Probably not: Congress has near-complete discretion to structure the appointment and removal provisions for the heads of agencies that it wishes to make independent.

B) Probably: The fact that the agency engages in prosecutions means that the President has inherent Article II authority to remove those ultimately responsible for such prosecution decisions.

C) Probably: Such immunization of agency heads from at-will removal makes them fundamentally unaccountable and thus unconstitutional under current Supreme Court authority.

D) Probably: Congress has a great deal of discretion to structure the appointment and removal provisions for the heads of agencies that it wishes to make independent, but normally Congress cannot reserve removal authority to itself.

43. One month after the agency publishes a notice of proposed rulemaking, one of the agency heads runs into the head lobbyist for the American Association of Bankers while the two are in a security line at Dulles Airport in Washington. During the course of the 20-minute delay, the lobbyist attempts to engage the agency head in a conversation about the proposed regulation, including passing him a document consisting of the association's talking points on the issue. The agency head attempts to resist the discussion, but the lobbyist's perseverance and the fact they are stuck in a line make that impossible. Which of the following statements about the impact of that conversation is/are true?

I. While normally the private party might be subject to adverse impacts from this *ex parte* communication, under the "honest servant" doctrine, the agency head's resistance to the communication removes that risk.

II. The agency head is obliged to place the document in the public rulemaking record.

III. Because this is a rulemaking, there is no formal prohibition on this communication unless the rulemaking involved "competing private claims to a valuable privilege."

A) II only.

B) III only.

C) I and II only.

D) I only.

44. Assume that during the pendency of the rulemaking, one of the agency heads gives a speech in which he castigates the mortgage underwriting industry, calling them "greedy sharks who were only too happy to write loans they should not have written, earning fees and then passing off the risks and leaving both borrowers and the securities markets holding the bag." The Association of Mortgage Lenders immediately sues, seeking to have that member of the agency disqualified from any role in the rulemaking on the ground that he is biased. What would be the result?

A) The association will probably lose unless it can show that the member had an "unalterably closed mind."

B) The association will certainly lose since no amount of prejudgment of an issue is unconstitutional for an agency that is charged with continual development of policy in a given area.

C) The association will probably win since prejudgment of broad legislative-type facts of this sort is particularly problematic, given that it involves prejudgment of broad social conditions affecting many individuals.

D) The association will certainly win because the context is rulemaking: prejudgment of the same types of facts in the course of an adjudication would not present a problem.

45. The agency finally promulgates a regulation limiting subprime lending. Which of the following statements best states the prevailing law about the standing to sue enjoyed by Stanley Paulson, a low-income individual who is currently in the market for a home loan?

A) Paulson would almost assuredly be within the zone of interests sought to be protected by the statute and thus would be able to sue so long as he met Article III's requirements.

B) So long as Paulson satisfied the Article III requirements for standing, then he could sue; the APA abrogates the "zone of interests" test that otherwise exists.

C) Paulson might or might not satisfy the zone of interests test, depending on the kinds of legal protection that the statute gave individual borrowers.

D) Paulson would probably satisfy the zone of interests test but not the separate standing test that courts have found implicit in the APA.

46. Assume that it becomes known that during the rulemaking process, the OMB funneled information from interest groups representing bankers to the agency via the OMB regulatory review process, and that that information was not placed on the public rulemaking record. To what extent would this fact affect Paulson's claim that the regulation should be overturned?

A) It would provide a further ground for overturning the regulation.

B) OMB review is not required in the case of informal rulemaking; thus, it would not help Paulson's challenge.

C) It would not help Paulson's challenge because executive orders dealing with regulatory oversight generally do not create legal rights that can be vindicated in court.

D) It would not affect Paulson's challenge either way because the court would probably dismiss such a claim as a political question.

47. Assume that the American Bankers' Association sues the agency, alleging that the regulation is arbitrary and capricious and harms its member banks. Which of the following statements about the association's standing is/are correct?

  I. The association can sue if it demonstrates that it is an effective litigant on behalf of bankers' interests, regardless of whether it showed that any of its members would have standing in their own right.

  II. The association could almost assuredly not ask for injunctive relief, but it could ask for damages.

  III. The association would need to demonstrate that the interests that it is protecting in the lawsuit are germane to the organization's purpose.

    A) I, II, and III.

    B) III only.

    C) I and III only.

    D) II only.

48. Assume that the press uncovers patterns of aggressive and potentially illegal mortgage lending practices by banks. A public interest group representing low-income people petitions the agency to commence a rulemaking regulating these practices. The agency refuses. Can the group challenge that refusal in court?

A) No: Decisions not to begin a rulemaking are presumptively unreviewable unless the authorizing statute provides criteria by which a court can judge the agency's refusal.

B) Yes: Courts generally require that agencies refusing such requests take a "hard look" at the option of commencing a rulemaking.

C) Yes: However, judicial review of such refusals is very deferential.

D) No: Article II's conferral to the President of power to execute the law means that courts cannot interfere when an agency refuses to commence a rulemaking to enforce the statute.

Questions 49–50 refer to the following situation.

Sam Francis has a license from the State of Kentucky to be a horse trainer. The state wishes to strip him of that license based on an allegation that he committed "a gross and unjustified act of cruelty" against a horse that he was training. Under the state law, such abuse renders the license holder liable to losing his license.

49. Which of the following, if true, would be relevant to the question whether Sam has a property interest in the license?

 I. Kentucky law provides that anyone who meets the relevant qualifications and pays the specified fee is entitled to a trainer's license.

 II. Horse training is a lucrative profession in Kentucky.

 III. Allegations of abuse such as those brought against Sam almost always turn on eyewitness testimony, which requires cross-examination for full ventilation of the issue.

 A) III only.

 B) I and III only.

 C) II and III only.

 D) I only.

50. Assuming Sam had a property interest in the license, which of the following would be relevant to the question of how much process is due?

 I. The procedures that the Kentucky licensing statute provides when the state seeks to strip someone of his trainer's license.

 II. Whether allegations of abuse such as those brought against Sam almost always turn on eyewitness testimony, which requires cross-examination for full ventilation of the issue.

 III. Whether training licenses were generally crucial to the economic well-being of people who made their living training horses.

 A) I, II, and III.

 B) II only.

C) II and III only.

D) I and III only.

51. Assume that after the next presidential election, the candidate from the party currently out of the White House wins — that is, there is a change of party control of the presidency. Assume further that labor regulations promulgated by the outgoing administration become final and go into effect on December 7 of the election year — six weeks before Inauguration Day. Upon taking office the following January 20, the new President's Secretary of Labor decides to rescind those regulations. An industry group challenges that rescission. What would be the result?

A) The court would not require any procedural formality or explanation from the agency since the agency would simply be rescinding its own regulation.

B) The amount of scrutiny that a court would give to the rescission would depend on whether the rescission amounted to deregulation or an increase in regulation. If the rescission tended to deregulate, then no process or explanation would be required. However, if it tended to increase regulation, then the agency would have to commence a new rulemaking procedure and provide a reasoned explanation for its regulatory choice.

C) Regardless of whether the rescission tended to deregulate or increase regulation, the agency would have to commence a new rulemaking procedure and provide a reasoned explanation for its regulatory choice.

D) The agency would be without the power to rescind the regulation without a "slate clearing" statute by Congress wiping out the earlier regulation.

52. Which of the following statements about ripeness and finality is/are true?

I. The Court has moved from a formalistic conception of these concepts toward a view that finds agency action more likely to be final and ripe for judicial review earlier in the regulatory process.

II. Congress has largely resisted judicial moves toward earlier judicial review of agency action, instead enacting statutes requiring that courts wait until an agency has actually enforced a regulation against a party.

III. Finality focuses only on the legal effect of the challenged action; any concern with whether the agency has reached a definitive conclusion on the issue is accounted for solely by the exhaustion doctrine.

A) I only.

B) III only.

C) I and II only.

D) I and III only.

Questions 53–55 refer to the following fact pattern.

A hypothetical federal statute, the "Federal Safe Electronics Act," authorizes the Consumer Products Safety Commission ("Agency") to promulgate regulations "after hearing, to ensure safe consumer electronics."

53. What procedures would a court require the agency to follow when promulgating regulations?

A) The term "after hearing" triggers the formal rulemaking requirements of APA Sections 556 and 557.

B) The term "after hearing" triggers only the informal notice-and-comment rulemaking requirements of APA Section 553. However, under current law, courts interpreting Section 553 may impose significant procedural requirements on the agency with regard to the content of the notice of the proposed rule and the content of the agency's statement explaining the basis and purpose of the final rule it settles on.

C) The term "after hearing" triggers only the informal notice-and-comment rulemaking requirements of APA Section 553. Under current law, courts interpreting Section 553 may impose only the most minimal procedural requirements on the agency.

D) The term "after hearing," because of its generality, is understood as a delegation of authority to courts to impose whatever procedures they think appropriate, in light of their estimation of the importance of the issue and the value of particular processes.

54. Assume that the agency engages in the rulemaking process. At the end of the process, it announces that it will promulgate a rule that is different from the proposed rule that it originally disclosed, explaining that the comments that it received led it to make the alterations. The Consumer Electronics Federation of America sues, alleging that it did not have a chance to comment on the final rule since it was different from the proposed rule that was the subject of the comment. Will it win its lawsuit?

A) No: So long as the final rule was "the logical outgrowth" of the proposed rule.

B) Yes: Any change in the rule between its proposed and final stages means that interested parties were denied the chance to comment.

C) No: Changes in rules between their proposed and final stages are to be expected, and, indeed, they suggest that the comments persuaded the agency. This indicates that the rulemaking process was a success, not that it needs to be restarted.

D) No: Under the "single stage" doctrine, a court reviewing a rulemaking process conducted in good faith, with the agency considering the comments it received, will not force the agency to recommence the process.

55. Assume instead that the agency decides to forego rulemaking in favor of bringing a series of adjudications accusing individual manufacturers of violating the statute. One of the manufacturers sues, challenging the agency's decision. How would a court analyze the challenge?

A) The court would use its independent judgment in determining whether the nature of the regulatory issue justified the agency's decision to use adjudications instead of rulemaking.

B) The court would defer completely to the agency's choice.

C) The court would start with a presumption that the agency should use rulemaking, and it would allow the agency to proceed immediately to adjudications only if the agency succeeded in overcoming that presumption.

D) The court would largely defer to the agency's choice but would consider whether the agency's decision to use adjudications imposed unfair retroactive liability.

56. The Board of Equalization of the State of Oregon has decided that, because of Portland's increasing attractiveness as a place to live, all property in Portland is undervalued for property tax purposes. It thereby announces a rule that, for property tax purposes, all property in that city will be revalued upward, by 30 percent. The board uses a process akin to the notice-and-comment process in APA Section 553, but when several property owners seek an oral hearing to present their objections to the plan, the board refuses the request. The property owners sue, alleging a violation of their procedural due process rights. Do they have a good claim?

A) Yes: While the state legislature might not have to provide individualized hearings when engaging in this type of conduct, an agency does.

B) Yes: Anytime government action significantly interferes with one's property interests, due process provides a right to an individualized hearing, even if the hearing is informal.

C) No: An agency acting under properly delegated power does not have to provide a hearing when it acts, even if its actions interfere with property interests.

D) No: The generally applicable nature of the decision (to all property in Portland) and its basis in general, legislative-type facts (the attractiveness of Portland as a place to live) mean that due process does not require the agency to provide individualized hearings.

57. Which of the following types of regulations are not mentioned as exceptions to some of or all the requirements for notice-and-comment rulemaking under the APA?

A) Rules relating to military and foreign affairs functions.

B) Procedural rules.

C) Rules with minimal economic or social impact.

D) General statements of agency policy.

58. Which of the following is **NOT** a consideration that courts use when evaluating an agency's claim that a particular rule is interpretive, rather than legislative, and thus did not have to go through the notice-and-comment process?

A) Whether the agency published the rule in the *Code of Federal Regulations.*

B) Whether without the rule, the agency would have any basis for bringing an enforcement action against a party.

C) Whether the rule amends or otherwise alters a previously promulgated legislative rule.

D) All three of these factors are relevant.

59. What is the rule with regard to *ex parte* contacts when an agency conducts a notice-and-comment rulemaking?

A) There is a strict rule in the APA restricting such contacts.

B) The APA contains no such rule, but under current judge-made administrative law, there is a strict limit on such contacts.

C) Such a rule, to the extent it exists, is limited only to special situations that are functionally closer to adjudications.

D) Such contacts are prohibited as violations of the Due Process Clause.

60. Assume that a regulatory statute authorizes the agency to adjudicate violations of a statute and whatever regulations the agency promulgates, but it also requires that the adjudicatory decisions be made "after hearing." How would a court probably evaluate whether the agency would have to comply with the APA's requirements for formal adjudication?

A) Because the statute does not include the "magic words" of "on the record after opportunity for agency hearing" the court, doing its own independent analysis of the statute, would find that the APA's formal procedures were not required.

B) Courts are generally more prone to find formal procedures required when an agency adjudicates regulations, as opposed to promulgating; thus, a court using its independent analysis would likely find this language to trigger the APA's formal requirements.

C) Unless the statute clearly resolved the issue of the need to use the APA's formal procedures, the court would defer to an agency's interpretation of the statute so long as that interpretation was reasonable.

D) Adjudications never have to follow requirements based in the APA; the only requirement is that the agency complies with procedural due process.

61. Assume that an agency is not required to follow the formal adjudication requirements in the APA. Does the APA impose any procedural requirements on the agency?

A) No: Any attempts to impose requirements not explicitly provided for in the APA would run afoul of the Supreme Court's caution in *Vermont Yankee* not to impose free-floating, nontextual procedural requirements.

B) Yes: The APA requires that agency actions (including adjudications) not be arbitrary or capricious; the Court has interpreted that requirement to mandate at least a minimal procedure so as to provide justifications for the agency action that can furnish the basis for that arbitrariness review.

C) Yes: The APA has an overall requirement that "agency procedures be appropriate to the importance of the issue decided," and this requirement has been used as a default procedural requirement when the APA's formal procedures are not required to be used.

D) Whenever the agency adjudicates the formal requirements of the APA are required.

62. Which of the following is **NOT** a requirement that the APA imposes for formal adjudications?

A) The right to have the proponent of the rule or order carry the burden of proof.

B) The right to have the transcript of the testimony and the exhibits be the exclusive record for decision.

C) A restriction on *ex parte* communications between the adjudicator and the agency-employee prosecutor.

D) All of the above are requirements for formal adjudications.

63. Which of the following is **NOT** a requirement that the APA imposes for formal rulemaking?

A) The right to have the proponent of the rule or order carry the burden of proof.

B) The right to have the transcript of the testimony and the exhibits be the exclusive record for decision.

C) A restriction on *ex parte* communications between the hearing officer responsible for promulgating the regulation and the agency employee who presents the case for the regulation.

D) All of the above are requirements for formal rulemakings.

64. In 2007, the Federal Trade Commission (FTC) submitted a report to Congress on the legality of pricing systems used by the semiconductor industry. The FTC wrote this report as part of its statutory obligations to keep Congress apprised of new developments relevant to the FTC's mandate to ensure fair conditions of trade in interstate commerce. The 2007 report concluded that the unit pricing method generally used in this industry likely violates federal fair trade laws. In 2011, the FTC brings an action against American Semiconductor, Inc. (ASI), a leading semiconductor manufacturer, alleging that its use of the unit pricing method violates federal trade laws. ASI moves to disqualify the agency heads from adjudicating the enforcement action, on the ground that they have prejudged the case in violation of its due process rights. What would be the result?

A) ASI wins so long as it can show that the FTC has an "unalterably closed mind" on the issue whether unit pricing violates federal law.

B) ASI wins so long as it can show that the FTC is likely to have prejudged the issue.

C) The fact that the FTC wrote the report to Congress concluding that unit pricing violates federal law establishes a presumption that the agency prejudged the issue; thus, ASI wins unless the FTC can rebut that presumption.

D) The FTC wins: The fact that Congress had given the FTC the power both to write reports and adjudicate claims based on those reports means that as a matter of law, the FTC cannot have unconstitutionally prejudged the issue.

65. In 2009, the FTC began an enforcement action against Universal Pharmaceutical, Inc. (UPI), alleging that it violated fair trade laws when it tied sales of its new wonder drug, Theramal, to sales of its older, less popular, anti-hypertension drug, Clotisone. UPI moved to disqualify the chair of the FTC from hearing the case on the ground that, 10 years ago, the current chair was the lead counsel to the Senate Committee that wrote a report concluding that UPI likely violated fair trade laws by insisting that hospitals buying Theramal also buy Clotisone. UPI argued that the chair's participation in reaching the Senate report's conclusion that UPI engaged in this conduct constituted unfair prejudgment that violated its due process rights. Which of the following statements about this motion is true?

I. A court would likely apply the same standard to this claim as it would to a claim that the agency had unconstitutionally prejudged a policy fact — that is, a fact about the pharmaceutical industry generally, rather than UPI's conduct in particular.

II. A court would likely ask whether the FTC head had an "unalterably closed mind" on the issue of UPI's conduct.

III. The fact that the agency was adjudicating an enforcement action, rather than drafting a regulation, would be irrelevant to the standard that the court would use when deciding UPI's claim.

IV. The fact that the chair of the FTC engaged in this past work history would not state any claim of prejudgment; all that matters is whether the chair's current work involved him in any unconstitutional prejudgment.

A) I only.

B) III only.

C) III and IV only.

D) II and III only.

66. The Rocktown Police Department circulates a flyer to all local businesses with the title "Active Shoplifters in Rocktown." The list advises businesspeople to beware of the people identified by name and photo on the flyer, calling them "known shoplifters active in the community." Sam Steadman is named on the list, and his "mug shot" is displayed. However, Sam has never been convicted of shoplifting, or any crime at all; he was arrested for shoplifting, but the charges were dropped when he produced the sales receipt for the item. Sam was never notified that the police were going to circulate the flyer; he found out when his employer was given one. Sam sues, alleging that he has been deprived of his good name, and thus of his liberty, without procedural due process. Assume that the common law of New Jefferson, the state where Rocktown is located, recognizes a tort cause of action for defamation. Which of the following statements best reflects the law governing his claim?

A) The existence of the tort cause of action indicates that Sam had an objectively reasonable expectation that his good name would not be impaired, and thus he has a liberty interest protected by due process.

B) While normally the existence of a tort cause of action would create an objectively reasonable expectation that his good name would not be impaired, the Supreme Court does not recognize a due process liberty interest simply in one's good name.

C) The existence of a tort cause of action is, in general, irrelevant to whether an individual has a due process protected liberty interest.

D) Sam may not have a liberty interest, but the definition of "property" in the Fourteenth Amendment's Due Process Clause probably includes his interest in his good name.

Questions 67–76 deal with the following situation.

Assume that the SEC brings an enforcement action against Stepford Brothers, a major investment bank, in which the agency accuses Stepford of violating the securities laws with regard to the company's involvement in derivatives markets. The agency uses the formal adjudication proceedings provided for in the APA.

67. After concluding the oral hearing, the ALJ realizes that she needs further information about the workings of a particular derivatives market. The ALJ walks down the hall of the SEC building to speak with one of the agency's economists. Under what circumstances can she do this?

A) Only if she gives notice of the meeting to the parties and gives them a chance to participate in the conversation.

B) She doesn't have to give notice to the parties and give them a chance to participate so long as the expert did not testify or otherwise participate in the adjudication process.

C) She doesn't have to give notice to the parties and give them a chance to participate since she is asking about a policy fact rather than a fact relating to Stepford's particular conduct.

D) There are no restrictions on her ability to have this conversation because she would be consulting with someone inside the agency.

68. After concluding the oral hearing, the ALJ realizes she may have misunderstood some of the testimony given by an agency expert. The ALJ walks down the hall of the SEC building to speak with the expert, to get clarification of his testimony. Under what circumstances can she do this?

A) She may not have this conversation under any circumstances because it would violate the integrity of the hearing process for her to reopen the hearing, even if she gave notice to the parties and a chance to participate.

B) Only if she gives notice of the meeting to the parties and gives them a chance to participate in the conversation.

C) She doesn't have to give notice to the parties and give them a chance to participate so long as she was simply seeking clarification of the witness's testimony rather than seeking new information.

D) There are no restrictions on her ability to have this conversation because she would be consulting with someone inside the agency.

69. Assume now that the case is decided by the ALJ without any *ex parte* contacts. The losing party appeals the decision to the heads of the agencies (the commissioners of the SEC). One of the commissioners wants to discuss a technical point about the economics of the derivatives markets. He wants to walk down the hall of the SEC building to speak about the issue to an agency economist who hasn't otherwise participated in the case. Under what circumstances can the commissioner do this?

A) Only if he gives notice of the meeting to the parties and gives them a chance to participate in the conversation.

B) He doesn't have to give notice to the parties and give them a chance to participate because of his status as the head of the agency.

C) He doesn't have to give notice to the parties and give them a chance to participate since he is asking about a policy fact rather than a fact relating to Stepford's particular conduct.

D) He cannot have this conversation under any circumstances because of his status as the head of the agency.

70. Assume now that the case is decided by the ALJ without any *ex parte* contacts. The losing party appeals the decision to the heads of the agencies (the commissioners of the SEC). In reading the transcript of the hearing, one of the commissioners wants to discuss a point with the agency's prosecutor. He walks down the hall of the SEC building to speak with the prosecutor. Under what circumstances can the commissioner do this?

A) Only if he gives notice of the meeting to the parties and gives them a chance to participate in the conversation.

B) He doesn't have to give notice to the parties and give them a chance to participate because of his status as the head of the agency.

C) He can have this conversation only if he wants to clarify a part of the record, not to elicit new information or arguments.

D) He cannot have this conversation under any circumstances because of his status as the head of the agency.

71. Assume now that even before the hearing is held by the ALJ, the attorney for Stepford discovers that the prosecutor in Stepford's case oversees the department where the ALJ works. Is this legal?

A) Yes.

B) Yes, so long as the relationship is disclosed.

C) Yes, although if the verdict is appealed to an Article III court, the agency would have to prove that there was no inappropriate influence.

D) No.

72. Assume now that the ALJ has decided the case without any *ex parte* contacts or supervisory relationship issues. The loser appeals the case to the agency heads (the commissioners of the SEC). Before the agency heads hear the appeal, the

attorney for Stepford discovers that the agency heads are the ultimate supervisors of the prosecutor. Is this legal?

A) Yes.

B) Yes, so long as the relationship is disclosed.

C) Yes, although if the verdict is appealed to an Article III court, the agency would have to prove that there was no inappropriate influence.

D) No.

73. Assume now that after conducting the hearing, the ALJ decides that she doesn't understand one of Stepford's arguments. She considers telephoning Stepford's attorney to obtain clarification. Under what circumstances can she do this?

A) Only if she gives notice of the meeting to the government lawyer and gives him a chance to participate in the conversation.

B) He doesn't have to give notice and a chance to participate to the government lawyer because this type of external *ex parte* contact is not restricted by the APA.

C) He can have this conversation only if he wants to clarify a part of the record, not to elicit new information or arguments.

D) He cannot have this conversation under any circumstances; once the hearing is concluded, it cannot be reopened.

74. Assume now that Stepford's attorney contacts the ALJ by phone to provide her with more information about Stepford's argument. The ALJ is unable to cut the attorney off before he provides significant information. What steps must the ALJ take?

A) She must rule against Stepford in the underlying litigation.

B) She must notify the agency head so he can make a decision whether to rule against Stepford in the underlying litigation.

C) She must disclose the substance of the *ex parte* communication.

D) She is not required to take any particular action.

75. Assume now that, rather than Stepford making the *ex parte* contact, it is the American Banking Association, a trade group that concerns itself with the promotion of the banking industry (including investment banks like Stepford). The ALJ is unable to cut the attorney off before he provides significant information. What steps must the ALJ take?

A) She must rule against Stepford in the underlying litigation.

B) She must notify the agency head so he can make a decision whether to rule against Stepford in the underlying litigation.

C) She must disclose the substance of the *ex parte* communication.

D) She is not required to take any particular action.

76. Assume now that Stepford is not engaged in an adjudication with the SEC but rather is participating in a formal rulemaking process. To what extent are the ALJ, agency personnel, Stepford, and other private parties subject to Section 554(d)'s restrictions on <u>intra-agency</u> *ex parte* contacts and Section 557(d)'s limitations on <u>external</u> *ex parte* contacts?

A) Both sets of restrictions apply.

B) Neither set of restrictions apply.

C) Section 554(d)'s limits on intra-agency *ex parte* contacts apply, but not Section 557(d)'s limits on external *ex parte* contacts.

D) Section 554(d)'s limits on intra-agency *ex parte* contacts do not apply, but Section 557(d)'s limits on external *ex parte* contacts do.

77. What is the standard by which courts review the policy judgments made by an agency in the course of an informal rulemaking?

A) The court asks whether the agency's decision was supported by substantial evidence.

B) The court asks whether it can hypothesize a rational basis for the agency's action.

C) The court asks whether the agency's action is arbitrary or capricious.

D) The court asks whether the agency's action is supported by a preponderance of the evidence.

78. Which of the following statements reflects the APA's provisions dealing with the reviewability of agency action?

I. Congress, if it wishes, can write a statute precluding judicial review of agency action.

II. If agency action is committed to agency discretion by law, then the agency action is unreviewable.

III. The only time the APA precludes judicial review is if a statute expressly precludes judicial review; if a statute is so broad that there is "no law to apply," then it is a violation of the nondelegation doctrine and the statute is unconstitutional.

IV. The APA reflects a presumption that agency action is not reviewable unless Congress expressly provides for judicial review.

    A) IV only.

    B) I and II only.

    C) I and III only.

    D) II and IV only.

79. The Immigration and Nationality Act requires the agency to take into custody aliens convicted of certain crimes and forbids release on bail. An alien taken into custody under this provision files a petition for habeas corpus, claiming that the blanket denial of bail to people in his situation violated due process. In defense, the agency cites the following provision from the statute:

> (e) *Judicial Review*
> The Attorney General's discretionary judgment regarding the application of this section shall not be subject to review. No court may set aside any action or decision by the Attorney General under this section regarding the detention or release of any alien or the grant, revocation, or denial of bond or parole.

Can the court hear the alien's petition?

A) Probably not: The Supreme Court has declared that statutes precluding judicial review will be given a broad reading, in deference to congressional control over the cases that federal courts may hear. Such a broad reading would result in the Court finding Congress to have precluded judicial review.

B) Probably not: The Supreme Court has declared that statutes precluding judicial review should be given their natural meaning, without any presumptions for or against judicial review. Such a reading of this statute would most likely result in the Court finding Congress to have precluded judicial review.

C) Maybe: The Supreme Court has declared that there is a presumption in favor of judicial review. Applying that presumption to this statute might result in the Court finding Congress to have not precluded constitutional claims of the sort made by the alien in this case.

D) Probably: The Supreme Court has declared that Congress has the power to preclude judicial review of agency action only in the rarest of circumstances, where unimportant rights are at stake. The importance of this right probably means that the Court would refuse to give effect to the statute's obvious preclusion of judicial review.

Questions 80–86 reflect the following situation.

Assume that Congress enacts a statute entitled the Shanksville National Monument Act, commemorating the spot in Pennsylvania where the fourth hijacked plane on 9/11 crashed. A key part of the statute reads as follows:

> The Department of the Interior shall manage the Monument area in a way that preserves the memory of those who died on 9/11, while also promoting peace, tolerance, and diversity.

80. A group of 9/11 survivors who visit the monument every year sues the department, alleging that its allowance of concession stands and video games in the monument area violates the statute's management mandate. The plaintiffs allege that the agency has failed to act in the way required by the statute. The department argues that the claim is not reviewable under the APA. What would be the result?

    A) The agency wins: The APA makes reviewable only discrete actions and failures to act, not failures to engage in ongoing action such as management of the monument.

    B) The agency wins: The APA makes reviewable both discrete and ongoing actions, but not failures to act, as alleged in the lawsuit.

    C) The agency loses: The APA expressly makes reviewable both discrete and ongoing actions and discrete and ongoing failures to act.

    D) The agency loses: The APA does not expressly define "agency action," but courts have interpreted that term to include both discrete and ongoing actions and discrete and ongoing failures to act.

81. Assume now that the survivors' group petitions the Department of the Interior to begin a rulemaking procedure that would address the specifics of how the monument should be managed. The agency declines the petition. Can the group sue, challenging the agency's refusal to begin a rulemaking procedure?

    A) No: Decisions to begin or not begin a rulemaking process are presumptively unreviewable.

    B) Yes: In deciding whether the agency acted inappropriately, the Court would take a "hard look" at the agency's regulatory options.

    C) Yes: However, the judicial review of the agency's decision would be extremely deferential.

    D) Yes: However, so long as the agency provided a reason for declining the petition, the court would uphold its decision.

82. Assume that after filing this lawsuit, the survivors' group makes a request under the FOIA seeking memos about the litigation strategy that the agency will use. Why would the court rule against this request?

A) Because FOIA requires a person requesting information to have a "legitimate use" for the information, and litigation against the agency itself is not considered a "legitimate use."

B) Because an exemption to FOIA for "memorandums and letters which would not be available by law to a party . . . in litigation with the agency" has been interpreted to preserve for the agency standard litigation privileges, such as the work-product privilege.

C) Because an exemption to FOIA for "information developed or created by the agency" has been interpreted to preserve for the agency standard litigation privileges, such as the work-product privilege.

D) Because based on case law, a court would likely find that this request satisfies FOIA's exemption for "other equitable reasons" for refusing disclosure.

83. Assume now that the survivors' group makes a request under the FOIA for any information relating to the agency's policies regarding food and video game concessions at the monument. What would be the result?

A) The agency would probably have to comply with the request: FOIA is a broad statute with exceptions only for national security and crime investigation information, neither of which would cover the information that the group is requesting.

B) The agency would probably have to comply with the request: FOIA is a broad statute whose exceptions would probably not cover the information that the group is requesting.

C) The agency would probably have to comply, but only if the group demonstrated to the agency that the information was necessary for its legitimate purposes.

D) The agency would not have to comply, given FOIA's exception for information "developed or created in the course of its ongoing statutory responsibilities."

84. Assume now that Concession Concepts (CC), the company that has the food concession at the monument, hears of the group's FOIA request and worries that the agency may disclose the details of its successful bid for the concession. It sues to enjoin the agency from disclosing that information. Which of the following best states the law governing that claim?

A) CC may bring a "reverse FOIA" suit seeking to enjoin disclosure of the information on the ground that disclosure would be arbitrary and capricious and/or violate some other provision of law.

B) CC may bring a "reverse FOIA" suit to make the argument, still undecided by the Supreme Court, that the exceptions to FOIA are mandatory — *i.e.*, that if a request falls within any FOIA exception, the agency is *prohibited* from disclosing the information.

C) CC may bring a "reverse FOIA" suit alleging that disclosure in this particular case would be inappropriate because the group has no legitimate need for the information.

D) CC may not bring a "reverse FOIA" suit on any ground.

85. Assume now that the survivors' group's FOIA request is opposed by the agency on the ground that it comes within the "trade secrets" exception to FOIA, since it necessarily asks for information related to the bids that concession companies have given to supply food at the monument. To what extent can the judge review the requested information in her chambers ("in-camera review"), to determine if the exception in fact applies?

A) The judge may not engage in this in-camera review because it would necessarily require the disclosure of the information, which would defeat the very purpose of the exception.

B) The judge may engage in this in-camera review, but only if the agency consents.

C) The judge may engage in this in-camera review, but only if the requester consents.

D) The judge may engage in this in-camera review without the consent of the parties.

86. Assume now that the survivors' group sues when the agency withholds some of the information requested, citing a FOIA exemption. According to the text of FOIA, which party has the burden of proof that the information does or does not fall within the claimed exemption?

A) The agency has the burden of proving that it does fall within the exemption.

B) The requesting party has the burden of proving that it does not fall within the exemption.

C) The matter is determined by the court without any burden on either side.

D) FOIA is silent on the burden of proof.

87. Matt Madigan is an intelligence analyst for the Central Intelligence Agency (CIA). He is also gay. When his supervisor discovers Matt's sexual orientation, he fires him. Matt sues, alleging that the CIA both violated the statute creating the CIA (which specifies the situations where analysts can be fired) and the Constitution, by discriminating against him based on sexual orientation. Which of the following statements most accurately states the law governing the reviewability of his two claims?

A) Under the doctrine of "pendant constitutional reviewability," a court would likely find Matt's statutory claim reviewable so long as it found his constitutional claim reviewable.

B) The Court would most likely strain harder to find Matt's constitutional claim reviewable, given the "serious constitutional questions" that arise when constitutional claims cannot be reviewed by a federal court.

C) The Court would most likely strain harder to find Matt's statutory claim reviewable, given that Congress is a constitutionally coequal branch of government.

D) The fact that the lawsuit involves the CIA probably means that the issue would be considered a political question.

Questions 88–93 refer to the following situation.

This year, Congress enacts a bill regulating global warming. The statute is a lengthy, complex document imposing a variety of duties on the Environmental Protection Agency (EPA) and giving it the power, among other things, to enact rules and prosecute violations of the statute and any regulations promulgated thereunder.

88. Assume that, before promulgating any regulations via the notice-and-comment process, the EPA publishes a "general statement of policy" that it states will guide its decisions about which enforcement actions to bring. Did it have to use notice-and-comment procedures before publishing it?

A) Yes, if the document binds the EPA in the sense that the EPA considers that prosecutorial personnel do not have discretion to deviate from the criteria noted in the document.

B) No, because the agency always has the ultimate discretion whether to use the notice-and-comment process.

C) Yes, because "general statements of policy" are subject to notice-and-comment requirements.

D) No, because courts have recognized a judge-made exception for policy statements.

89. Assume that Crow Chemical, a major chemical manufacturer, sues the agency, alleging that the policy reflects a misreading of the statute. Under what circumstances can it sue now, rather than waiting for an enforcement action against it?

A) Crow could never sue now: such a lawsuit would not constitute a case or controversy and thus would violate Article III.

B) Crow could sue now only if the agency itself permitted the lawsuit, under the doctrine of "permissive jurisdiction."

C) Crow could sue now if the issue was one that was amenable to judicial review in the absence of further factual developments, and if the private party would suffer significant hardship from having to wait for an enforcement action.

D) Crow could sue now without having to satisfy any particular test.

90. Assume that Crow can sue now, and that the regulation it challenges is in fact a general statement of policy, promulgated without a notice-and-comment process. Which of the following statements best reflect(s) current law about the deference the agency's interpretation would receive from a court?

   I. The fact that the interpretation was not reached as a result of notice-and-comment procedures means that it would receive no deference at all.

   II. The fact that the interpretation was not reached as a result of notice-and-comment procedures means that it would receive whatever deference would be appropriate under the concept of *Chevron* deference.

   III. Whether the interpretation was reached as a result of notice-and-comment procedures is irrelevant to the type of deference that it would receive.

   A) I only.

   B) II only.

   C) III only.

   D) Neither I, II, nor III.

91. Assume that the agency's statutory interpretation made in the general statement of policy discussed in the past several questions does not receive *Chevron* deference, and that a court rules against the agency on the interpretive issue. The following month, the agency engages in a formal adjudication that would merit *Chevron* deference under *United States v. Mead Corp.*, 533 U.S. 218 (2001), and interprets the statute in the same way it had earlier — the same way that was rejected by the court in the prior case. When appealing its conviction in that adjudication to the same court that decided the earlier case, the defendant argues that the agency's interpretation should not get *Chevron* deference. What would be the result?

   A) The court would give *Chevron* deference. The fact that a court previously rejected a *Chevron*-ineligible interpretation does not affect the fact that *Chevron* deference is appropriate when the agency's interpretation qualifies for such deference.

   B) The court would give *Chevron* deference, but only if it found the statute "unusually opaque," a situation that creates a special reason for *Chevron* deference.

C) The agency would **NOT** give *Chevron* deference. The existence of the earlier court decision would prevent the court from giving *Chevron* deference in the subsequent case; otherwise, it would be allowing the agency to overrule the court.

D) The agency would **NOT** give *Chevron* deference. Once an agency uses a *Chevron*-ineligible format for acting (such as via a general policy statement), it has lost its opportunity to get *Chevron* deference in later cases, even when it otherwise would be called for.

92. Assume now that the agency promulgates a regulation through a manner other than notice-and-comment rulemaking. The regulation simply repeats the statutory language. The agency then interprets the regulation. When a party sues, alleging that the agency mistakenly interpreted that regulation, the agency argues that its interpretation should get the type of deference due when an agency interprets its own regulation (so-called *Seminole Rock* or *Auer* deference). Is the agency correct?

A) No: There is no deference customarily accorded to an agency's interpretation of its own regulation.

B) Yes: Agencies get deference when they interpret their own regulations, and the agency would receive that deference in this case.

C) No: An agency's interpretation of its own regulations, like all agency interpretations, either get *Chevron* deference or *Skidmore* deference but no other type.

D) No: Normally, an agency gets deference when it interprets its own regulation, but not when an agency enacts a regulation that simply parrots statutory language with the goal of gaining deference for an interpretation that would otherwise not merit it.

93. Assume now that the statute at issue was enacted in 1970, rather than this year. In 1979 (before *Chevron* was decided), the agency argued to the First Circuit Court of Appeals that its interpretation of the statute, reached via a formal adjudication, was correct, but the First Circuit disagreed. In 2009 (after *Chevron* was decided), the agency again interpreted the statute in a formal adjudication and reached the same interpretation that the appellate court rejected 30 years earlier. This time, however, the agency argued that it should win under *Chevron*. Assume that the Court correctly concluded that the statute is unclear on the precise interpretive issue. What would be the result?

A) The agency wins: Under the "last in time" doctrine, the agency is allowed to overrule an earlier contrary appellate court decision so long as the agency's interpretation qualifies for *Chevron* deference.

B) The agency wins: In such a situation, the appellate court must examine its 1979 opinion. If that opinion concluded that the statute was unclear on this precise issue, then the court must rule for the agency.

C) The agency loses: Even though the agency would win if there was no relevant precedent, the existence of the 1979 pre-*Chevron* decision interpreting the statute in a particular way is still good law unless explicitly overruled by the appellate court.

D) The agency loses unless it can prove to the court that the statute is clear.

94. Sometimes judicial review of agency policymaking is described as a "hard look" review. What does this term mean?

A) Agencies must take a "hard look" at the regulatory problem.

B) The Supreme Court must take a "hard look" at an appellate court's reasoning when it reviews agency policymaking, to ensure that the court did not overstep its boundaries.

C) The regulated community must take a "hard look" at an agency's proposed resolution of a problem (either a proposed adjudicative result or a proposed regulation).

D) Congress must take a "hard look" at an agency's regulation before deciding to reverse it via a statute.

95. When a court is reviewing agency policymaking, when does it review the action for "substantial evidence"?

A) When the agency action is informal.

B) When the agency action is formal.

C) When the agency action is on an "especially important matter."

D) When the agency taking the action is an independent agency.

96. What is generally considered the difference between an "arbitrary and capricious" review and a "substantial evidence" review?

A) A "substantial evidence" review is stricter.

B) A "substantial evidence" review is more deferential.

C) A "substantial evidence" review requires a court to base its decision solely on the public record made by the agency.

D) An "arbitrary and capricious" review requires a court to base its decision solely on the public record made by the agency.

97. Bobby Badguy is incarcerated in a maximum-security federal prison. The prison manual states that inmates are entitled to eat with the other

prisoners so long as there is no lockdown or other security issue, and so long as the inmate follows prison rules. One day, he is told that he will be fed alone for one month because he broke prison rules by waving a fork in a threatening manner. Bobby sues, alleging that due process requires a hearing before he is confined to his cell at mealtime. Which of the following rules best describes how a court would analyze his claim?

A) Prisoners have no procedural due process rights, as those rights are considered to have been part of the "liberty" that is surrendered upon conviction and incarceration.

B) Bobby probably does have a liberty interest protected by due process, given the entitlements set forth in the manual.

C) Bobby has a liberty interest only if a court decides that the deprivation at issue is "atypical and significant."

D) Bobby would have a liberty interest, given the entitlements set forth in the manual, but only if he showed that he had actually read the manual.

98. In the small town of Dusty, New Mexico, a justice of the peace adjudicates speeding fines. Under New Mexico law, a town is allowed to keep half the fines from speeding tickets and is further authorized to forward any part of its share of the fines as compensation for the justice of the peace. A Dusty ordinance provides that one-quarter of its share of speeding fines shall be given to the justice of the peace as compensation for his or her services. Is this arrangement constitutional?

A) No, if a particular speeder can prove that the justice of the peace was biased by the prospect of receiving extra money in that particular speeder's case.

B) No, if a particular speeder can prove that, in general, the justice of the peace was biased by the prospect of receiving extra money.

C) No. The justice of the peace's obvious personal interest in convicting alleged speeders is enough for this scheme to constitute a due process violation, in the absence of any proof.

D) Yes: despite the seeming bias, judges are irrebuttably presumed unbiased unless they are convicted of bribery or another crime of dishonesty.

99. Which the following statements most accurately describes when government has deprived a person of a due process-protected interest?

A) A deprivation occurs whenever the government agent is responsible for the interest being lost.

B) A deprivation occurs only if the government agent acted with malice.

C) A deprivation occurs only if the government did not give notice that it was planning on denying the interest.

D) A deprivation occurs only if the government agent acted intentionally to deny the interest.

100. Which of the following statements most accurately states the rule governing the requirement that individuals challenging agency action must first exhaust their administrative remedies?

A) This rule is strictly enforced by courts as a part of Article III's case-or-controversy requirement.

B) This rule is strictly enforced by courts as a prudential matter, not an Article III matter.

C) Exhaustion is the general rule, but the rule is subject to exceptions.

D) The exhaustion requirement has been abandoned by federal courts, though it remains in effect in many state courts.

ADMINISTRATIVE LAW
MULTIPLE CHOICE
100 ANSWERS AND ANALYSIS

ADMINISTRATIVE LAW ANSWERS AND ANALYSIS

1. Issue: Legislative Veto

The correct answer is **D**, which reflects the rule from *INS v. Chadha*, 462 U.S. 919 (1983). In *Chadha*, the Court struck down a statutory provision that authorized one house of Congress to "veto" a proposed agency action. The Court held that this "legislative veto" allowed Congress to legislate in ways that fell short of the bicameralism and presentment required by Article I of the Constitution. The two-house veto in this question is also a legislative veto; it satisfies the bicameralism requirement, but not presentment to the President, and thus it would be unconstitutional. Answer A is therefore incorrect. Answer B is incorrect because Congress can in fact require that regulations not take effect for a particular period of time; indeed, Section 553(d) of the APA provides that regulations do not generally become valid until 30 days after publication in the *Federal Register*. Answer C is incorrect because Congress may enact laws that undo regulations; it's just that those laws must be real laws — *i.e.*, laws enacted via the bicameralism and presentment process.

2. Issue: Nondelegation Doctrine

The correct answer is **B**, which reflects the results of cases alleging unconstitutional delegations of legislative power. In only two cases from 1935 has the Supreme Court ever struck laws down as violating the nondelegation doctrine; since then, it has upheld exceptionally broad delegations of power. See, *e.g., Whitman v. American Trucking Associations*, 531 U.S. 457 (2001), collecting cases. Answer A is incorrect because it suggests tougher nondelegation review than is actually the case; in many cases, statutes upheld against nondelegation challenges have not fully resolved basic policy tradeoffs. Answer C is incorrect because the statutes struck down in 1935 were delegations of legislative, not adjudicatory, power. See *Panama Refining Co. v. Ryan*, 293 U.S. 388 (1935); and *A.L.A. Schecter Poultry Corp. v. United States*, 295 U.S. 495 (1935). Answer D is incorrect because the statute clearly requires the agency to do more than simply make factual findings; however, that fact does not doom the statute to being struck down on nondelegation grounds.

3. Issue: Rulemaking Procedures

The correct answer is **B**. The statute requires the agency to promulgate rules "after hearing"; this terminology falls short of the "magic words" standard ("on the record after opportunity for an agency hearing") that the Court held was generally the prerequisite for requiring formal rulemaking in *Florida East Coast RR v. United States*, 410 U.S. 224 (1973). Thus, only informal, notice-and-comment rulemaking would be required. Answer A is incorrect because *Mathews*-style due process analysis would not apply to a rulemaking procedure. See generally *BiMetallic Inv. Co. v. State Bd. of Equalization*, 239 U.S. 441

(1915), explaining when due process applies. Answer C is incorrect because oral hearings are features of formal rulemakings, which the agency would not have to follow here, under *Florida East Coast*. Answer D is incorrect because the Supreme Court in *Vermont Yankee Nuclear Power Corp. v. Natural Resources Defense Council*, 435 U.S. 519 (1978), held that courts could not use their own freestanding conceptions of how much process an agency should use when engaging in rulemaking.

4. Issue: Procedures for Notice-and-Comment Rulemaking

Items I and III are the only parts of the correct answer; thus, answer **C** is correct. I is correct because in cases such as *Nova Scotia Food Products Corp. v. United States*, 568 F.2d 240 (D.C. Cir. 1977), the courts have held that adherence to notice-and-comment procedures requires the agency to disclose to interested parties the data on which the agency was basing its analysis. II is incorrect because the Supreme Court in *Vermont Yankee Nuclear Power Corp. v. Natural Resources Defense Council*, 435 U.S. 519 (1978), held that courts could not use their own freestanding conceptions of how much process an agency should use when engaging in rulemaking, including how much process in light of the court's estimation of the importance of the issue being decided. III is correct because in cases such as *Natural Resources Defense Council v. U.S. E.P.A.*, 279 F.3d 1180 (9th Cir. 2002), courts have held that if the notice-and-comment process changes the agency's mind so much that the final rule is not the "logical outgrowth" of the original proposed rule, then the agency must restart the process to give interested persons a chance to comment on the agency's new proposal. IV is incorrect because due process analysis does not to apply to rulemaking. See generally *BiMetallic Inv. Co. v. State Bd. of Equalization*, 239 U.S. 441 (1915), explaining when due process applies.

5. Issue: *Ex Parte* Contacts in Rulemaking

The correct answer is **A**. The only restrictions on *ex parte* communications in rulemaking are those enshrined in Section 557(d) of the APA. Those restrictions, however, deal with *ex parte* contacts between the ALJ and parties *outside* the agency; thus, they don't apply to this fact pattern. The restrictions on this communication reflected in the other answer choices are therefore all incorrect.

6. Issue: Prejudgment of the Issue in Rulemaking

The standard for when an agency decision maker has prejudged an issue to be considered in a rulemaking is whether the decision maker has an "unalterably closed mind." See *Association of National Advertisers v. FTC*, 627 F.2d 1151 (D.C. Cir. 1979). Thus, answer **B** is correct. Answer A is incorrect because it states the wrong standard. Answer choice C essentially assumes that the decision maker would have to recuse himself or herself on the threshold question of whether to impose these limits; again, such recusal is necessary only if he or she has an unalterably closed mind. Answer D is incorrect because it states too strong a rule: Even though the "unalterably closed mind" standard is hard for a challenger to satisfy, it still offers him or her the chance of meeting it and forcing recusal.

7. Issue: Exceptions to the Rulemaking Process

The correct answer is **C**. Answer C reflects the rule that an agency that foregoes notice-and-comment rulemaking by invoking the policy statement exception to the process will have to litigate challenges to the policy decision inherent in that statement when it seeks to apply it in an enforcement action. See, *e.g., American Mining Congress v. Mine Safety & Health Administration*, 995 F.2d 1106 (D.C. Cir. 1993), explaining this general rule. Answer A is incorrect because "general statements of policy" are exempt from the notice requirement of Section 553 (and hence from the comment that follows that notice); see 5 U.S.C. Section 553(b). For this same reason, answer D is incorrect. Answer B is incorrect because it is not the case that courts generally reject agencies' claims that a particular statement is exempt from the rulemaking process as a general policy statement.

8. Issue: The Timing of Challenges to a Rule

The correct answer is **C**, which states the rule from *Abbott Labs v. Gardner*, 387 U.S. 136 (1967), that pre-enforcement review of agency action is generally available unless Congress explicitly precludes it or the court determines that additional facts are necessary to illuminate the legal issue. See also *Toilet Goods Ass'n v. Gardner*, 387 U.S. 158 (1967); court holds that additional facts would illuminate the issue better and thus refusing pre-enforcement review of the agency action. Answer A is incorrect because *Abbott Labs* makes clear that sometimes pre-enforcement review cases can be heard by courts and thus satisfy the case-or-controversy requirement of Article III. Answer B is incorrect because the default is in favor of pre-enforcement review, not against it, as suggested by this answer. Answer D is incorrect because it goes too far: Hardship to the private party is one of the factors in the *Abbott Labs* analysis, but not the only one; thus, a showing of hardship does not mean that pre-enforcement review will necessarily be allowed.

9. Issue: Standing to Challenge a Rule

The correct answer is **C**. Associations have a special, three-part, standing test: (1) at least one member must have standing; (2) the subject of the lawsuit must be germane to the association's interests; and (3) the relief sought must be effective in the absence of the individual injured member as a named plaintiff [*Hunt v. Washington State Apple Advertising Comm'n*, 432 U.S. 333 (1977)]. A citizen-suit provision is unnecessary; thus, answer A is incorrect. Similarly, the existence of the associational standing test means that answer D is incorrect, or at least not a very good answer. The question, then, is which of these three requirements, if any, may Congress abrogate? In *United Food and Commercial Workers v. Brown Group*, 517 U.S. 544 (1996), the Supreme Court held that the first prong is constitutionally based (which means that Congress cannot abrogate it), but the third is merely prudential, which means Congress can abrogate it. Thus, answer B is incorrect and answer C is the correct answer.

10. Issue: The "Zone of Interest" Standing Requirement

The correct answer is **D**. Section 702 of the APA states, in relevant part, that "A person suffering legal wrong because of agency action, or adversely affected or aggrieved by agency action within the meaning of the relevant statute, is entitled to judicial review thereof." In *Association of Data Processing Service Organizations v. Camp*, 397 U.S. 150 (1970), the Court held that this language allowed plaintiffs to have standing (assuming they satisfied Article III's requirements) so long as they were "arguably within the zone of interests sought to be protected by the statute." Answer A is incorrect because the direct or indirect nature of the plaintiff's injury is not relevant to standing. Answer B is incorrect because Section 702 imposes the zone of interests test, which, while easy to satisfy, is nevertheless a prudential barrier to standing. Answer C is incorrect because the zone of interests test does not require an investigation into whether the plaintiff lobbied Congress for passage of the statute that it is now seeking to challenge.

11. Issue: Sources of Federal Court Jurisdiction to Hear Challenges to Agency Action

Only item II is correct; thus, **C** is the correct answer. I is wrong because APA Section 704 does not itself confer jurisdiction on the federal courts to hear challenges to agency action. III is wrong because the doctrine of federal pendent jurisdiction is irrelevant to federal courts' jurisdiction to hear challenges to federal agency action. II is correct; Section 1331, the general federal question jurisdiction statute, does provide federal courts with jurisdiction to hear challenges to federal agency action since those challenges present questions of federal law.

12. Issue: Deference to Agency Statutory Interpretations

The correct answer is **B**, which correctly states the rule from *Chevron USA v. Natural Resources Defense Council*, 467 U.S. 837 (1984). Under the *Chevron* test, the Court first determines whether the statute clearly answers the question at issue, using "traditional tools of statutory construction." If the court finds a clear meaning, it applies it. If the court can't, it will defer to any reasonable agency interpretation of the statute. This second step of the process means that answer C is wrong. Answer A is wrong because most judges will do at least some examination of the legislative history of a statute, as part of their use of "traditional tools of statutory construction," when determining whether a statute clearly answers the question. Answer C is wrong because the court has applied the *Chevron* case to agency regulations; indeed, *Chevron* itself concerned a regulation.

13. Issue: Review of Agency Policy-Making

Only item II is correct; thus, answer **C** is correct. Item II is part of the test that courts use when applying this standard. See, *e.g., Motor Vehicle Mfrs Ass'n v. State Farm Ins. Co.*, 463 U.S. 29 (1983). Item I is incorrect because under the arbitrary and capricious standard, courts will not hypothesize possible rationales for the agency's action. See, *e.g., State Farm*. Item III is incorrect because courts have understood this standard to require that the agency's action be justified by any information in the agency's possession, not just the public record. See *Citizens to Preserve Overton Park v. Volpe*, 401 U.S. 402 (1971). Other cases have required the agency to expand its public record, but *Overton Park* still contemplates that the agency's action may be upheld "based on the full administrative record that was before [the agency] at the time [of its decision]." Item IV is wrong because the arbitrary and capricious standard applies to notice-and-comment rulemaking. See, *e.g., State Farm*.

14. Issue: *Ex Parte* Contacts During White House Rulemaking Review

The correct answer is **D**. Since the Clinton administration, the executive orders overseeing administrative agencies have restricted these types of *ex parte* communications. However, they do not prohibit them; hence, answer A is incorrect. Even more to the point, even if they did prohibit them, the orders make clear that they do not create rights that are enforceable in court; thus, a court could not use such a violation as a reason for striking down an agency action. This latter fact makes answer D correct. Answer B is wrong because it states that in general, *ex parte* contacts with personnel outside the agency are not regulated by the APA in the context of rulemaking; this is incorrect, as Section 557(d) imposes such limits on formal rulemaking. Answer C is wrong because there is no such thing as harmless error review in judicial review of agency processes under the APA.

15. Issue: Existence of a Due Process-Protected Interest

The correct answer is **B**, which states the rule from *Bd of Regents v. Roth*, 408 U.S. 564 (1972), that property interests are defined by reasonable expectations created by a legal source, such as state or federal law. Here, if the federal veterans statute establishes eligibility criteria for benefits, then it creates a reasonable expectation in those benefits that therefore constitutes due process "property." Answer A is incorrect because it considers the importance of the interest; this is a factor in determining how much process is due, not whether it is a property interest to begin with. (But note that the answer is doubly wrong in that even on this latter issue, the importance of the interest must be defined on a classwide basis, not on the basis of the individual recipient's case.) Answer C is incorrect because it refers to the amount of process provided by the government, which again is relevant to the "How much process is due?" issue, not the "Is there a due process property interest at stake?" issue. Answer D is incorrect because, like answer A, it speaks to the importance of the benefit, which is not a factor in determining whether it constitutes a due process–protected property interest.

16. Issue: The Amount of Process Required Under Due Process

Answer **C** is the best answer and therefore is correct. Answer C reflects the three-part test established by *Mathews v. Eldridge*, 424 U.S. 319 (1976), to determine how much procedure is protected by due process. That test balances the importance of the benefit to the class of recipients, the government's interest, and, as indicated in this answer, the risk of error inherent in the current procedures and the improvement in accuracy that could be expected from the requested procedures. Answer A is incorrect because *Mathews* recognized that due process is a flexible concept whose requirements will vary from situation to situation. Answer B is incorrect because it reflects the idea of the "bitter with the sweet" — *i.e.*, the notion that government can use the same expectations analysis used to create property interests to condition the amount of process that the individual can reasonably expect. The Supreme Court rejected this idea in *Cleveland Bd of Education v. Loudermill*, 470 U.S. 532 (1985); today, the amount of process that is due is determined by the court, without any recourse to what the individual could be led to expect by the statute. Answer D is incorrect; while in some cases, courts seem to give somewhat less protection to statutorily granted "new property" rights as compared with traditional common-law rights, this is not the law. At any rate, D is not as good an answer as C, which accurately states the formal law today.

17. Issue: Due Process Doctrine

The correct answer is **D**. The concept of the "new property" holds that due process should protect more than interests traditionally protected by the common law, to protect other interests, such as professional licenses and government benefits, that people have reasonably come to rely on. See *Bd of Regents v. Roth*, 408 U.S. 564 (1972); and *Goldberg v. Kelly*, 397 U.S. 254 (1970), explaining this theory. Answer A is wrong; the doctrine of "the bitter with the sweet" was rejected in *Cleveland Bd of Education v. Loudermill*, 470 U.S. 532 (1985). Answer B is not the best answer; while some courts have focused on personal dignity in considering how much process is due, the dominant test in this area, announced in *Mathews v. Eldridge*, 424 U.S. 319 (1976), essentially amounts to a social welfare maximization test examining the importance of the interest, the government's interest in avoiding additional procedures, and the increased decisional accuracy that would flow from more elaborate procedures. Answer D is unambiguously correct, and thus a better answer. Answer C is incorrect because the due process inquiry is split into several components, including whether there is a due process interest at stake, and, if so, how much process is due (see *Roth*).

18. Issue: Agency Discretion to Choose Between Rulemaking and Adjudication

The correct answer is **B**, which reflects the rule that agencies have a great deal of discretion to choose whether to proceed by rulemaking or adjudication, though that discretion is not absolute. See, *e.g., NLRB v. Bell Aerospace*, 416 U.S. 267 (1974). This rule means that answer A is incorrect because it does not reflect that agency discretion, while broad, is not absolute. Answer C is incorrect because while this fundamental fairness rule has been adopted in the Ninth Circuit [see *Ford Motor v. FTC*, 673 F.2d 1008 (9th Cir. 1981)], it is not the rule elsewhere and the Supreme Court has never embraced it. Answer D is incorrect because it suggests a level of judicial second-guessing of the agency's choice between rulemaking and adjudication that is inconsistent with the *Bell Aerospace* rule.

19. Issue: Reviewability of Agency Prosecutorial Decisions

The correct answer is **A**, which states the rule from *Heckler v. Chaney*, 470 U.S. 821 (1985), that agency decisions not to prosecute are presumptively unreviewable. Congress can overcome that presumption with clear language directing how the agency should use its prosecutorial discretion, but there is no such language in this statute. For this reason, answers B and C are incorrect. Answer D is incorrect because it applies the zone of interest test for standing, which is not the issue here. If it were, this test would be easy for plaintiffs to meet. See, *e.g., National Credit Union Admin. v. First National Bank and Trust*, 522 U.S. 479 (1998).

20. Issue: Presidential Authority to Control Agency Heads

The correct answer is **D**. The facts of this case mirror those in *Humphrey's Executor v. United States*, 295 U.S. 602 (1935), where the Court upheld Congress's immunization of an agency official from at-will firing by the President. However, the analysis in that case has been superseded by the Court's analysis in *Morrison v. Olson*, 487 U.S. 654 (1988), where the Court used the test reflected in answer D to uphold the immunization of the special prosecutor from at-will removal by the President, despite the prosecutor's obvious performance of executive functions. This fact makes answer A incorrect. Answer B is incorrect because *Morrison* still applies a test, which presumably might be used to strike down a future congressional attempt to immunize a different agency official. Answer C is incorrect because *Morrison* makes clear that there would be a constitutional problem if Congress tried to retain the removal power for itself, rather than simply taking it away from the President.

21. Issue: Reviewability of Agency Prosecutorial Decisions

The correct answer is **B**, which reflects the rule from *Heckler v. Chaney*, 470 U.S. 821 (1985), that agency decisions not to prosecute are presumptively unreviewable. This fact makes answer D incorrect. Answer A is incorrect because the plaintiff would probably have standing; all that would be required, other than Article III standing, is that the plaintiff be "arguably within the zone of interest sought to be protected by the statute." This is an easy test to meet. See *National Credit Union Admin. v. First National Bank and Trust Co.*, 522 U.S. 479 (1998). Answer C is incorrect because 28 U.S.C. Section 1331, the general federal question jurisdiction statute, would normally provide jurisdiction for a suit like this.

22. Issue: Required Rulemaking Processes

The correct answer is **C**. Answer A is incorrect because due process generally does not apply to rulemaking. See *BiMetallic Inv. Co. v. State Bd of Equalization*, 239 U.S. 441 (1915), explaining when due process applies. Answer B is incorrect because only the APA's informal notice-and-comment requirements would apply here; the statute does not contain the "magic words" ("on the record after opportunity for agency hearing") that the Court has said are essentially required before formal rulemaking procedures (including oral hearings) are required. See *Florida East Coast RR v. United States*, 410 U.S. 224 (1973). This combination means that answer C is correct. Answer D is incorrect because "hard look" review is review of the substance of the agency's action, not the procedures that it used; at any rate, under *Vermont Yankee Nuclear Power Co. v. Natural Resources Defense Council*, 435 U.S. 519 (1978), courts may not impose more procedural requirements than those entailed in the APA.

23. Issue: Standing to Challenge Agency Action

The correct answer is **B**, which identities the legal test and predicts the likely outcome. In addition to satisfying Article III requirements, a plaintiff seeking to sue an agency must satisfy the zone of interests test courts have imposed as an interpretation of APA Section 702. Thus, answer A is incorrect. This is an easy test to meet [see, *e.g., National Credit Union Admin. v. First National Bank and Trust Co.*, 522 U.S. 479 (1998)]. Thus, answer D is incorrect. Answer C is incorrect because the legal right test has been abandoned in favor of the zone of interests test.

24. Issue: Deference to Agency Statutory Interpretations

The correct answer is **A**, which states the correct rule from *Chevron USA v. Natural Resources Defense Council*, 467 U.S. 837 (1984), on how a court reviews an agency's interpretation of its statute. Answer B is incorrect because due process is irrelevant to this issue; at any rate, the court has rejected the idea that "pure questions of law" are not subject to *Chevron*. Answer C is incorrect; a holding that the statute does not answer the precise question simply means that *Chevron* deference is used, not that the issue is unreviewable as committed to the agency's discretion. Answer D is incorrect, because the two-step *Chevron* test described in answer A assumes that a holding that the statute does not precisely answer the question does not necessarily mean that the statute is an unconstitutional delegation of legislative power.

25. Issue: Congressional Review of Agency Action

The correct answer is **C**, which reflects the prohibition on legislative vetoes announced in *INS v. Chadha*, 462 U.S. 919 (1983). Section 5 is a legislative veto, as it allows Congress to change legal rights without going through the full bicameralism and presentment process. Thus, answers A and B are incorrect. Answer D is incorrect because there's no problem with the statute delaying the effect of regulations promulgated by the agency; even in the APA, Congress did this by requiring that regulations not become effective until 30 days after their publication in the *Federal Register* [see 5 U.S.C. 553(d)].

26. Issue: Deference Standards for Agency Statutory Interpretations

The correct answer is **B**. In *United States v. Mead Corp.*, 533 U.S. 218 (2001), the Court held that an agency's authority to engage in rulemaking suggested congressional intent to delegate the power to act with the force of law. In addition, to the extent that the agency actually used that power, the interpretation would be considered to have the force of law—that is, it would receive *Chevron* deference. Answer A is incorrect because under this analysis, *Skidmore* deference would normally apply only if the agency did not use this sort of authority to interpret the statute — that is, if it acted by means short of a rulemaking (or formal adjudication). Answer C is incorrect because, as indicated above, it is relevant whether the agency interpreted the statute via a rulemaking process. Answer D is incorrect because the *Mead* Court did not distinguish between formal and informal rulemaking.

27. Issue: The Constitutionality of Agency Adjudication Procedures

Answer **C** reflects the combination of correct items, and thus is the correct answer. Item I is incorrect because this type of argument could be styled as a due process claim, as well as a claim about the separation of powers. See, *e.g., CFTC v. Schor*, 478 U.S. 833 (1986). This fact makes Item II part of the correct answer. Item III is also part of the correct answer because the standards of review in this statute are similar to those noted with favor in *Schor*. Item IV is incorrect because this right—based on a statute, creating a right running between a private party and the federal government—is a paradigmatic example of a public right. Public rights are generally allowed to be adjudicated in agency courts with no Article III problem (*see Schor*). This fact also makes item V incorrect.

28. Issue: Intra-Agency *Ex Parte* Contacts in Adjudication

The correct answer is **D**. This fact pattern is governed by Section 554(d), which sets forth restrictions on *ex parte* communications in the course of formal adjudications. (This is a formal adjudication because the statute states that the adjudications be "on the record after opportunity for an agency hearing.") Section 554(d) says that an ALJ "may not . . . consult a person or party on a fact in issue, unless on notice and opportunity for all parties to participate." The expert would be a "person" the ALJ wishes to "consult" "on a fact in issue," and thus the communication could be done only with notice to both parties and a chance for them to participate. Answer D reflects this rule. This rule also makes answers A, B, and C incorrect.

29. Issue: Agency Heads' *Ex Parte* Contacts in Adjudication

The correct answer is **B**. As discussed in the analysis of the previous question, Section 554(d) restricts ALJs' ability to ask these types of questions. However, that same section of the APA states that its restrictions do not apply to agency heads. Thus, answer B is correct and answers A and D are wrong. Answer C is wrong because the statute imposes different restrictions on ALJs and agency heads, with the former more restricted in their ability to ask this type of question to this person. The fact that ALJs and agency heads face different restrictions makes C incorrect.

30. Issue: Formality Requirements for Agency Rulemaking

The correct answer is **B**, which states the rule that oral hearings are generally not required for rulemaking unless Congress specifies the "magic words" quoted in this answer. See *Florida East Coast RR v. United States*, 410 U.S. 224 (1973). Answer A is incorrect because due process would not apply in a rulemaking proceeding. See generally *BiMetallic Inv. Co. v. State Bd of Equalization*, 239 U.S. 441 (1915). Answer C is incorrect because under the informal rulemaking procedures, the agency need not make a finding that oral hearings were unnecessary; rather, the default is simply a paper hearing. Answer D is incorrect because it uses the wrong "magic words." To trigger the APA's formal rulemaking process a statute must say more than that the agency must act "after hearing" (see *Florida East Coast*).

31. Issue: *Ex Parte* Contacts During White House Rulemaking Review

Under the executive orders overseeing agency action in force since the Clinton administration, answer **A** is correct. Those orders require OMB to disclose into the public rulemaking record any information passed to in *ex parte* by persons outside the executive branch. See, *e.g.*, Exec. Order 12866, Section 6(b)(4). This requirement makes answers B, C, and D incorrect.

32. Issue: Extensions of Comment Periods in Rulemaking

Answer **C** is correct, as it accurately states the rule from cases such as *Natural Resources Def. Council v. U.S. EPA*, 279 F.3d 1180 (9th Cir. 2002), which require the agency to extend the rulemaking process when the comments the agency receives leads it to change its proposed rule so much that the new rule is not the "logical outgrowth" of the original proposed rule. This rule makes answer A incorrect. Answer B is incorrect because this rule is not derived from express language in the APA addressing extensions of comment periods (which does not exist), but rather from the general requirement that interested parties have a real opportunity to comment on proposed agency actions. As suggested by the date of the *NRDC* case, this rule survived the holding in *Vermont Yankee Nuclear Power Corp. v. NRDC*, 435 U.S. 519 (1978), that courts should not impose on agencies additional procedures above those required by the APA itself. Thus, answer D is incorrect.

33. Issue: Judicial Review of Agency Rulemaking

The correct answer is **D**, which accurately states the review that a court would give of the agency's regulation. The court would consider the process that the agency used, keeping in mind the rule from *Vermont Yankee Nuclear Power Corp. v. NRDC*, 435 U.S. 519 (1978), that courts must not impose additional requirements beyond those imposed by the APA. This latter fact makes answer B incorrect. A court would also give a potentially searching review of the substance of the agency's action. This fact makes answer A incorrect. Combined, these two facets of the court's review make answer D correct. Answer C is incorrect because under *Citizens to Preserve Overton Park v. Volpe*, 401 U.S.

402 (1971), the agency could defend its regulation based on any information it had, not just the information that it disclosed to the public.

34. Issue: Associational Standing

Only item IV is correct; thus, answer **B** is correct. I is wrong because Congress does in fact have the authority to abrogate this factor in the associational standing test. See *Food and Commercial Workers Union v. Brown Group*, 517 U.S. 544 (1996). II is wrong because it has the law backward; one of the requirements of association standing is that one of its members has standing to sue. See *Hunt v. Washington State Apple Advertising Comm'n*, 432 U.S. 333 (1977). III is wrong because it again has the law backward; injunctions are the paradigmatic example of the kind of relief that associations *can* request. IV is correct because it reflects the rule from *Brown Group*, noted above.

35. Issue: Freedom of Information

The only correct item is III, which means that answer **B** is correct. I is incorrect because the Supreme Court has accepted the concept of a "reverse FOIA" suit of this sort. See *Chrysler Corp. v. Brown*, 441 U.S. 281 (1979). *Chrysler* also held that because FOIA is a disclosure statute, the fact that certain information falls within an exemption does not mean that the agency is *required* to refuse disclosure; thus, II is incorrect as well. However, *Chrysler* did hold that a decision to disclose might be arbitrary or capricious, or in violation of some other law; thus III is correct. FOIA does not distinguish, as a general matter, between government-generated and government-acquired information; thus items IV and V are incorrect.

36. Issue: Fourth Amendment-Based Limits on Agency Inspections

The correct answer is **C**, which states the rule and likely outcome here. In *Camara v. Municipal Court*, 387 U.S. 523 (1967), the Supreme Court held that the Fourth Amendment does apply to administrative inspections. However, the Court has recognized an exception to the warrant requirement for closely regulated businesses, on the theory that they have diminished expectations of privacy due to their closely regulated nature. See *Colonnade Catering Corp. v. United States*, 397 U.S. 72 (1970). Thus, answer A is incorrect because it focuses on the wrong type of Fourth Amendment warrant exception—the "exigent circumstances" exception that is normally associated with criminal searches, rather than *Colonnade*'s "closely regulated business" exception. Answer B is incorrect because, as explained above, the Fourth Amendment does apply to administrative searches; moreover, there is no APA-based freedom from administrative searches. Answer D is incorrect because the Fourth Amendment does apply, even if exceptions are made. Answer C correctly reflects both the application of the Fourth Amendment and the exception for a business like a gun shop. See also *United States v. Biswell*, 406 U.S. 311 (1972), applying the "closely regulated business" exception to a gun dealer.

37. Issue: The Constitutionality of Agency Adjudication Schemes

Only item II is part of the correct answer; thus, answer **D** is correct. I is incorrect because under *Commodity Futures Trading Comm'n. v. Schor*, 478 U.S. 833 (1986), the stringency of the Article III court review of the agency's findings and conclusions is relevant to the statute's constitutionality. II is correct because in *Schor*, this factor cut in favor of the constitutionality of the administrative adjudication scheme that the agency court's orders could be enforced only by an Article III court. III is incorrect because while *Schor* de-emphasized the centrality of the private–public rights distinction for determining the constitutionality of agency adjudication schemes, that distinction is still one factor that a court must consider. IV is incorrect because appeal to an agency head is irrelevant to the issue; the real question is the availability of review by an Article III court and the scope and intensity of that review.

38. Issue: Intra-Agency *Ex Parte* Contacts in Adjudication

The correct answer is **B**. This question is governed by APA Section 554(d), which restricts *ex parte* communications during formal agency adjudications. (This is a formal adjudication because the statute requires that the result be reached "only the record after opportunity for agency hearing," the "magic words" that trigger formal adjudication.) Section 554(d) states than an ALJ "may not . . . consult a person or party on a fact in issue, unless on notice and opportunity for all parties to participate." The personnel that ALJ wants to "consult" are "persons" who would be "consult[ed] . . . on a fact in issue;" thus, 554(d) would allow the consultation, but only after the ALJ gave both parties notice and a chance to participate. Thus, answer A is incorrect since the notice requirement would apply even if the person consulted had not performed in the case as a prosecutor or witness. Answer C is incorrect because the consultation would have to include the notice and opportunity to participate restrictions noted above. Answer D is incorrect because the ALJ is not prohibited from having the conversation, so long as it's conducted with the statutory requirements satisfied.

39. Issue: The Exhaustion Requirement

The correct answer is **D**. Normally, exhaustion is required. See, *e.g., McCarthy v. Madigan*, 503 U.S. 140 (1992). However, courts sometimes make exceptions to that requirement (see *McCarthy*). Because courts sometimes make exceptions, answers A and B are incorrect. Answer C is incorrect because it conflicts with the general rule requiring exhaustion.

40. Issue: Judicial Review of Agency Prosecutorial Decisions

The correct answer is **A**, which accurately states the rule from *Heckler v. Chaney*, 470 U.S. 821 (1985) that agency decisions to prosecute are presumptively unreviewable. This rule makes answers B and C incorrect. Answer D is incorrect because Congress may, if it wishes, direct the agency to use its prosecutorial discretion in such defined ways that the agency's failure to do so would be subject to judicial review. See, *e.g., Dunlop v. Bachowski*, 421 U.S. 560 (1975); example of failure to prosecute being held subject to judicial review.

41. Issue: Statutory Specifications for Rulemaking Procedures

The correct answer is **C**. Here, the statute uses the "magic words" ("on the record after opportunity for agency hearing") to describe the process by which the agency must promulgate regulations; these words trigger the formal rule-making procedures of the APA. See *Florida East Coast RR v. United States*, 410 U.S. 224 (1973). Thus, answer B is incorrect. Answer D is incorrect because in *Vermont Yankee Nuclear Power Corp. v. Natural Resources Defense Council*, 435 U.S. 519 (1978), the Supreme Court held that courts could not require that agencies provide more rulemaking procedures than those set forth by the APA. Answer A is incorrect because due process does not apply to rule-making procedures. See *BiMetallic Inv. Co. v. State Bd of Equalization*, 239 U.S. 441 (1915).

42. Issue: Presidential Control over Agency Heads' Tenure

The correct answer is **D**, which states the rules developed in the Supreme Court's modern separation of powers jurisprudence, in particular *Morrison v. Olson*, 487 U.S. 654 (1988) and *Mistretta v. United States*, 488 U.S. 361 (1989). These cases make clear that Congress has a great deal of discretion to limit the President's power to remove agency officials, but that it may not reserve that removal power to itself, all as indicated by answer D. Answer A is close, but is not the best answer because it leaves open the possibility of Congress reserving removal power for itself. Answer D is more complete on that score, and its wording ("a great deal of discretion" versus "near-complete discretion") more faithfully reflects the limits on that power. Answer B is wrong because the Court in *Morrison* rejected basing its removal-power decision on whether the agency is engaged in executive powers or quasi-legislative powers. This distinction had been the rule from *Humphrey's Executor v. United States*, 295 U.S. 602 (1935), but *Morrison* cast severe doubt on that approach. Answer C is wrong because it overstates the limits on Congress to immunize agency personnel from presidential removal at will.

43. Issue: External *Ex Parte* Contacts and the Rulemaking Process

Only item II is part of the correct answer; thus, the correct answer is **A**. This question is governed by 5 U.S.C. Section 557(d), which restricts *ex parte* contacts between agency decision makers and personnel outside the agency when the agency is engaging in formal rulemaking or adjudication, as it is here, given the use of the "magic words" ("on the record after opportunity for agency hearing") to describe the rulemaking process that the agency must follow. Item I is incorrect because there is no such doctrine. II is correct because Section 557(d) requires the decision maker to place on the public record any information given to him in an *ex parte* communication. III is incorrect because Section 557(d) applies both to formal adjudication and formal rulemaking. See Section 557(a) (setting forth when the rest of that section applies).

44. Issue: Prejudgment of Issues in Rulemaking

The correct answer is **A**, which correctly identifies the "unalterably closed mind" standard for when due process requires a decision maker to recuse himself or herself in the course of a rulemaking where he or she is alleged to have prejudged legislative-type facts such as the general conduct of an industry. See *Association of National Advertisers v. FTC*, 627 F.2d 1151 (D.C. Cir. 1979). Answer B is incorrect because while this standard is hard for a plaintiff to meet, it does exist and therefore imposes at least a theoretical limit on decision makers' prejudgment. Answer C is incorrect because it has the relationship backward; in general, it is thought more problematic when decision makers prejudge adjudicative-type facts (*i.e.*, facts about a particular party), since the party itself is thought likely to have superior information about its own conduct, making prejudgment particularly problematic. Moreover, agencies are in the business of forming opinions about broad legislative-type facts (*i.e.*, facts about general social conditions), so prejudgment of those facts is generally thought not to present as serious a problem. Answer D is incorrect, both because it is often thought that it is the nature of the facts prejudged rather than the vehicle used by the agency (rulemaking or adjudication) that is relevant. Moreover, even if that were not the case, prejudgments in the course of an adjudication might be thought more problematic (in contradiction to this answer) since in general due process requires more protections in adjudication and less in rulemaking (see, *e.g., National Advertisers*).

45. Issue: "Zone of Interest" Standing

The correct answer is **A**. In addition to Article III requirements, APA Section 702 requires that a plaintiff challenging agency action be "arguably within the zone of interests sought to be protected by the statute." Here, Paulson would assuredly be within that zone, given the statute's obvious concern for individual borrowers. The zone of interests standard is not hard to meet. See *National Credit Union Admin. v. First National Bank and Trust*, 522 U.S. 479 (1998). Answer B is incorrect because APA Section 702 *imposes* the zone of interests requirement; it does not abrogate it. Answer C is incorrect because the zone of interests test is quite easy to meet, and given the focus of the statute on protecting individual borrowers, Paulson would surely satisfy it. Answer D is incorrect because the zone of interests test is the only standing test imposed by the APA; moreover, it is not an additional test derived from a source other than the APA.

46. Issue: Reviewability of Violations of OMB Rulemaking Review Procedures

The correct answer is **C**, as it states the correct rule. The executive orders dealing with regulatory oversight generally do not create rights that can be vindicated by a court. This fact makes answer A incorrect. Answer B is incorrect because it assumes that it does create such rights; moreover, these orders generally do apply to informal rulemaking, at least significant ones. Answer D is incorrect because the claim would not be a constitutional one for which the political question doctrine would be appropriate.

47. Issue: Associational Standing to Challenge a Rule

Only item III is correct; hence, answer **B** is correct. I is not correct because the associational standing test requires that at least one member of the group have standing to sue [*e.g., Hunt v. Washington State Apple Advertising Comm'n*, 432 U.S. 333 (1977)]. II is not correct because another component of the associational standing test is that the relief requested by the association must be effective in the absence of the individual member who would otherwise have standing (*Hunt*). This is generally thought to preclude an association for asking for damages, but to allow it to ask for an injunction. III is correct because the third *Hunt* requirement is that the association proves that the subject of the lawsuit is germane to the interests of the association.

48. Issue: Reviewability of Agency Refusals to Amend a Rule

The correct answer is **C**, which reflects the rule from *American Horse Protection Ass'n v. Lyng*, 812 F.2d 1 (D.C. Cir. 1987). In *American Horse*, the Court held that the characteristics of a decision to decline to initiate a rulemaking (*i.e.*, the relative rarity of rulemakings and their primarily legal focus) distinguish them from refusals to prosecute, which are presumptively unreviewable under *Heckler v. Chaney*, 470 U.S. 821 (1985). Moreover, the fact that Section 553(e) of the APA authorizes persons to petition an agency to commence a rulemaking suggests that an agency's decision to decline that petition should be reviewable. However, the court also stated that such judicial review is extremely deferential. Because these decisions are reviewable, answers A and D are incorrect. Answer B is incorrect because the review that a court does of such a denial is very deferential, not rigorous.

49. Issue: Identification of Due Process-Protected Interests

Only item I is correct; thus, **D** is the correct answer. I is correct because the Kentucky law creates an objectively reasonable expectation that someone who satisfies the statutory criteria will receive the benefit (the license); under the analysis in *Bd of Regents v. Roth*, 408 U.S. 564 (1972), this means that Sam would have a property interest in his license. II is incorrect because the importance (or in this case, desirability) of the benefit is irrelevant to the question whether Sam has a property interest in the license, even though it might be relevant to the question of how much process would be due before he could be stripped of his license. III is incorrect because this fact also goes to the question of how much process is due, under the analysis in *Mathews v. Eldridge*, 424 U.S. 319 (1976).

50. Issue: Determination of How Much Process Is Required by Due Process

Items II and III are the only correct ones; thus, answer **C** is correct. Item I is incorrect because the state cannot influence the amount of process that is due by creating an expectation in the statute that a beneficiary will get only a certain amount of process if he or she is deemed ineligible. The Court rejected this theory, sometimes called "the bitter with the sweet," in *Cleveland Bd of Education v. Loudermill*, 470 U.S. 532 (1985). II is correct because this fact goes to how much more accurate a decision might be expected to be if it included an oral hearing; this question of increased accuracy is a factor in the three-part test set forth by *Mathews v. Eldridge*, 424 U.S. 319 (1976), which is used to determined how much process is constitutionally due. III is correct because another factor in the *Mathews* test is the importance of the interest to the class of recipients.

51. Issue: Judicial Review of Agency Decisions to Reverse Course

The correct answer is **C**. After a regulation goes into effect, it can be rescinded only if the agency commences an entirely new rulemaking process, and the resulting amendment or rescission itself satisfies review under the arbitrary and capricious standard of review. That review would not be any more or less lenient than the review of the original regulation. See *FCC v. Fox Television Stations*, 129 S.Ct. 1800 (2009). This makes answers A and B incorrect. However, no action from Congress is required before the agency can begin the process of amending or rescinding a regulation. Thus, answer D is incorrect.

52. Issue: The Ripeness and Finality Requirements

Only item I is correct; thus, answer **A** is the correct answer. Item I is correct because courts have been moving away from rigid, formal requirements of ripeness and finality toward more functional approaches that turn on the actual status of the agency action and its amenability to judicial review. See, *e.g., Abbott Labs v. Gardner*, 387 U.S. 136 (1967), ripeness; and *Bennett v. Spear*, 520 U.S. 154 (1997), finality. Item II is incorrect because in fact, Congress tends to favor pre-enforcement review, to allow an early test of the agency's regulation to resolve questions about its legality. Item III is incorrect because in *Bennett*, the Court held that finality turned both on the legal effects of the challenged agency action and whether that action marked the culmination of the agency's decision-making process.

53. Issue: Statutory Specification of Rulemaking Procedures

The correct answer is **B**. Answer A is incorrect because in *United States v. Florida East Coast Ry. Co.*, 410 U.S. 224 (1973), the Supreme Court held that Congress must use the precise words "on the record after opportunity for agency hearing" if it wishes to require the agency to follow the APA's requirements for formal rulemaking. Thus, this statute requires only informal rulemaking. However, courts in cases such as *United States v. Nova Scotia Food Products Corp.*, 568 F.2d 240 (1977), have interpreted the APA's informal rulemaking procedures to require significant procedural care. Thus B is the correct answer and C is incorrect. D is incorrect because the sort of free-floating judicial discretion to insist on a particular level of procedural formality was explicitly disapproved by the Supreme Court in *Vermont Yankee Nuclear Power Corp. v. Natural Resources Defense Council, Inc.*, 435 U.S. 519, (1978).

54. Issue: Reopening Comment Periods in Rulemaking

The correct answer is **A**. The key question that courts ask when considering whether changes between an agency's proposed and final rules deprived parties of the right to comment is whether the final rule was "the logical outgrowth" of the proposed rule. The idea is that in such a case, the party could have foreseen that the proposed rule might evolve into the final rule, and thus it would be charged with the responsibility for commenting appropriately in the first round of rulemaking. See, *e.g.*, *Natural Resources Defense Council, Inc. v. U.S. Environmental Protection Agency*, 279 F.3d 1180 (9th Cir. 2002). This rule means that answers B, C, and D are incorrect. B would impose an impossible burden on the agency, requiring it to restart a rulemaking process anytime the comments that it received convinced it to make even a minor change in the rule. C is unfair to parties who would have no reason to comment on a regulatory approach not even suggested by the proposed rule, if the comments that the agency receives prompts it to change its approach completely. D is incorrect because there is no such "single stage" doctrine.

55. Issue: Agencies' Discretion to Choose Between Rulemaking and Adjudication

The correct answer is **D**, which best states the rule from cases such as *Securities and Exchange Commission v. Chenery Corp.*, 332 U.S. 194 (1947), and *N.L.R.B. v. Bell Aerospace Co. Div. of Textron, Inc.*, 416 U.S. 267 (1974). Answer A is incorrect because it implies too large a role for the courts in second-guessing the agency's choice of regulatory vehicles. Answer C is incorrect for the same reason. Answer B is incorrect because the complete deference that it reflects is too strong; even cases such as *Chenery* and *Bell Aerospace* suggest that an agency's choice between rulemaking and adjudication may in rare instances constitute an abuse of the agency's discretion.

56. Issue: When Individualized Hearings Are Required

The correct answer is **D**. This question reflects the relevant facts from *Bi-Metallic Inv. Co. v. State Bd. of Equalization*, 239 U.S. 441 (1915), a foundational case where the Court set forth when agency action triggers due process requirements. Under *BiMetallic*, agency action that is general in nature (rather than targeted at a particular individual) and based on general facts (rather than facts specific to a particular party) does not trigger the requirements of procedural due process. A is incorrect, as it suggests that due process does apply. B is incorrect, as it is too broad; it suggests that even legislative action impairing property interests triggers due process, which is a rule that the Court has never adopted. C is incorrect because it is also too broad; it suggests that agency action never triggers due process so long as it is based on delegation of legislative authority. This rule would essentially mean that agencies never had to comply with due process.

57. Issue: Exceptions to Notice-and-Comment Rulemaking

The correct answer is **C**. Section 553 of the APA does not exempt these sorts or rules from any part of the requirements for notice-and-comment rulemaking. Rules relating to foreign affairs functions are exempt under Section 553(a) from all the requirements of Section 553; thus, A is incorrect. Under Section 553(b), "rules of agency organization, procedure, or practice" are exempt from the requirement of notice (and hence, comment); thus, B is incorrect. That same subsection also exempts from the notice requirement "general statements of policy"; thus, D is also incorrect.

58. Issue: Distinguishing Legislative and Interpretive Rules

The correct choice is **D**. While the Supreme Court has not definitively decided this issue, appellate courts have identified all three of these factors as being relevant to the interpretive/legislative rule question. See, *e.g., American Mining Congress v. Mine Safety Health Administration*, 995 F.2d 1106 (D.C. Cir. 1993).

59. Issue: *Ex Parte* Contacts in Rulemaking

The correct answer is **C**. While cases such as *Home Box Office v. FCC*, 567 F.2d 9 (1977) initially imposed stringent limits on such contacts, subsequent cases, most notably *Vermont Yankee v. NRC*, 435 U.S. 519 (1978) cautioned courts not to impose more procedural requirements than those in the APA (which doesn't include restrictions on *ex parte* contacts in informal rulemaking). Currently, courts impose such limits, at most, when there are at stake "conflicting private claims to a valuable privilege"; that is, when the issue at stake is of a more classically adjudicative nature, with two parties claiming the same benefit. C reflects these developments, and thus is correct.

60. Issue: When Formal Adjudication Is Required

The correct answer is **C**, which states the general rule that the meaning of a statute's procedural requirements is a matter left to the agency's interpretation under the *Chevron* test. See, *e.g., Chemical Waste Mgt, Inc. v. US EPA*, 873 F.2d 1477 (D.C. Cir. 1989). B used to enjoy some adherence in the lower courts [see, *e.g., Seacoast Anti-Pollution League v. Costle*, 572 F.2d 872 (1st Cir. 1978)]; again, though, after *Chevron*, this approach has largely been abandoned. A is not correct because it both ignores *Chevron* and, even before *Chevron*, states a rule in tension with the *Seacoast* rule. D is incorrect because the APA does include formal procedural requirements for adjudication; the only question is when an agency is required to follow those formal procedures.

61. Issue: The APA's Requirements for Informal Adjudication

The correct answer is **B**, which states the rule from *Pension Benefit Guaranty Corp. v. LTV Corp.*, 496 U.S. 633 (1990). A states the general principle from *Vermont Yankee*, but in *Pension Benefit*, the Court recognizes this small caveat to the *Vermont Yankee* rule. C is incorrect, as there is no such language in the APA. D is incorrect because agency adjudications do not necessarily have to follow the APA's formal requirements.

62. Issue: The Requirements of Formal Adjudication

The correct answer is **D**. Sections 554, 556 and 557 provide the rules for formal adjudications. A is wrong because the burden of proof allocation is provided by Section 556(d). B is wrong because the right to a decision based solely on the record is protected by Section 556(d). C is wrong because the *ex parte* communication ban is found in Section 554(d). Thus, all these procedural protections are provided for formal adjudication, and D is the correct answer.

63. Issue: The Requirements of Formal Rulemaking

The correct answer is **C**. Sections 556 and 557 provides procedures for formal rulemaking. A is wrong because the burden of proof allocation is provided by Section 556(d). B is wrong because the right to a decision based solely on the record is protected by Section 556(d). C is the correct answer because the *ex parte* communication ban is found in Section 554(d), which applies only to formal adjudications, not rulemakings. (A separate protection against *ex parte* contacts applies to formal rulemakings, but it deals only with *external ex parte* contacts.) Because Section 554(d) does not apply to rulemakings, D is also incorrect.

64. Issue: Agency Prejudgment of Legislative Facts

The correct answer is **A**. These facts mirror those in *FTC v. Cement Institute*, 333 U.S. 683 (1948). In *Cement Institute*, the Court concluded that unless the minds of the decision makers were "irrevocably closed" by their prior conclusions in the report to Congress, due process did not require the decision makers to recuse themselves because of prejudgment. B is incorrect because it states too lenient a standard; this standard may be more appropriate for claims that an agency has prejudged an adjudicative fact (that is, a fact about a particular party's own unique conduct) rather than a policy fact (*e.g.*, that a particular pricing method is illegal). See, *e.g., Cinderella Career and Finishing Schools v. FTC*, 425 F.2d 583 (D.C. Cir. 1970); see also *United Steelworkers v. Marshall*, 647 F.2d 1189 (D.C. Cir. 1981), distinguishing between adjudicative facts and policy facts for purposes of prejudgment claims and requiring the plaintiff to show an "unalterably closed mind" before ruling in its favor on a claim of prejudgment of policy facts. C is incorrect for the same reason. D is incorrect because it goes too far in the other direction by making it impossible for a plaintiff to establish a due process violation because of prejudgment of policy facts. *Cement Institute* makes such claims hard to win, but not impossible.

65. Issue: Agency Prejudgment of Adjudicative Facts

The correct answer is **B**, since option III is the only one of the four that is correct. Option I is incorrect because prejudgment claims are normally decided based on different standards depending on whether the allegedly prejudged fact is adjudicative (that is, relating to the party's own unique conduct) or policy-related (that is, relating to general social facts unrelated to any one party's unique conduct). See *United Steelworkers v. Marshall*, 647 F.2d 1189 (D.C. Cir. 1981), distinguishing between adjudicative facts and policy facts for purposes of pre-judgment claims. Option II is incorrect because claims of prejudgment of adjudicative facts (such as UPI's own conduct) are judged under the "entrenchment" standard (asking if the decision maker is "entrenched" in his position, rather than the "unalterably closed mind" standard, which is harder for a plaintiff to meet). See *United Steelworkers*, distinguishing between these two standards. Option IV is incorrect because sometimes claims of unconstitutional prejudgment are successful when the prejudgment arose because of the decision maker's past work for another institution. See, *e.g.*, *American Cyanamid Co. v. FTC*, 363 F.2d 757 (D.C. Cir. 1966); a fact pattern where prejudgment occurred due to the decision maker's past work for a congressional committee. However, option III is correct because if the agency is prejudging policy facts, the standard is the same whether that prejudgment is made in the context of a rulemaking or an adjudication. Compare *United Steelworkers*, applying "unalterably closed mind" standard in the context of a rulemaking, *with FTC v. Cement Institute*, 333 U.S. 683 (1948), applying the essentially identical "irrevocably closed mind" standard in the context of an adjudication.

66. Issue: The Status of Reputation as a Due Process-Protected Interest

The correct answer is **B**. This case is based on the facts of *Paul v. Davis*, 424 U.S. 693 (1976). In *Paul*, the Court refused to find that the plaintiff had a due process–protected liberty interest in his good name, on the theory that "mere defamation" was insufficient to constitute such an interest. Thus, A is incorrect. However, in general, the Court's methodology for determining whether one has a property or liberty interest includes examining whether a law (including common law rules) gives an individual an objectively reasonable expectation of the benefit protected by the law [*e.g., Bd of Regents v. Roth*, 408 U.S. 654 (1972)]. Thus C is incorrect. Answer D is incorrect because while "liberty" in the Fourteenth Amendment has its own distinct meaning, "property" does not. B reflects the correct synthesis of these rules.

67. Issue: Intra-Agency *Ex Parte* Contacts in Adjudication

The correct answer is **A**, which accurately reflects the rule from Section 554(d) of the APA, which governs internal *ex parte* contacts in formal adjudications. The relevant part of Section 554(d) states that the ALJ "may not . . . consult a person or party on a fact in issue, unless on notice and opportunity for all parties to participate." By its terms, the expert would be a "person" the ALJ wants to consult "on a fact in issue;" thus, the ALJ would have to give notice before having that conversation. B is incorrect because another part of Section 554(d) deals with *ex parte* contacts with personnel who participate in the adjudicatory process; a non-testifying person is covered by the part of the statute covered above. C is incorrect because while other institutional integrity doctrines may turn on the type of issue being discussed, Section 554(d) does not. D is incorrect because Section 554(d) comprises a set of restrictions on ALJs' ability to have *ex parte* contacts with other agency employees.

68. Issue: Intra-Agency *Ex Parte* Contacts in Adjudication

The correct answer is **B**, which accurately reflects the rule from Section 554(d) of the APA, which governs internal *ex parte* contacts in formal adjudications. The relevant part of Section 554(d) states that "[a]n employee or agent engaged in the performance of investigative or prosecuting functions for an agency in a case may not, in that or a factually related case, participate or advise in the decision, recommended decision . . . except as witness or counsel in public proceedings." The witness here would be understood as having "engaged in the performance of an investigative or prosecuting functions" and thus, as the rest of the section states, could participate only as a "witness . . . in public proceedings" (*i.e.*, proceedings where notice and opportunity to participate were given to the parties). A is incorrect, as it is too draconian; nothing in the APA prohibits a reopening of the proceedings, so long as both sides get notice and a chance to participate. C is incorrect because this section of the APA does not distinguish between merely clarifying testimony and eliciting new information; indeed, any attempt to do so would be fraught with ambiguity, given that any clarification almost by definition elicits new information. D is incorrect because Section 554(d) comprises a set of restrictions on ALJs' ability to have *ex parte* contacts with other agency employees.

69. Issue: Intra-Agency *Ex Parte* Contacts with Witnesses in Adjudication

The correct answer is **B**, which accurately reflects Section 554(d)'s special rules for agency heads. Section 554(d) makes it clear that the restrictions that it imposes on ALJs do not apply to agency heads. Thus, answer A, which accurately states the rule that an ALJ would have to follow, is not correct here. C is incorrect, as Section 554(d) does not rely on a policy fact-adjudicative fact distinction. D is incorrect; it is right in that it notes that the adjudicator's status as an agency head matters, but it resolves that difference in the wrong direction — an agency head has *more*, not *less*, authority than an ALJ to have this conversation.

70. Issue: *Ex Parte* Contacts Involving Agency Heads in Adjudication

The correct answer is **A**, which reflects Section 554(d)'s rules for agency heads. Section 554(d) imposes restrictions on prosecutors and witnesses, in addition to adjudicators. The focus of those restrictions on the non–adjudicators presumably means that they apply regardless of whether the adjudicator is an ALJ or the agency head. Those restrictions prohibit persons participating in an adjudication as a prosecutor or witness from participating in the adjudication except in that capacity "in public proceedings." The requirement of a public hearing is reflected in answer A. B is incorrect because it suggests that those restrictions don't apply when it's the agency head acting as the adjudicator; as explained above, this is incorrect. C is incorrect because Section 554(d) doesn't draw this distinction, which at any rate would be very difficult to draw, given that clarifications almost by definition elicit new information. D is incorrect because it suggests that his status as the agency head imposes a special disability on his ability to ask this question. That is incorrect; as explained above, these restrictions apply regardless of who the agency adjudicator is.

71. Issue: APA Limits on Agency Structure

The correct answer is **D**. Section 554(d) states that an ALJ "may not . . . be responsible to or subject to the supervision or direction of an employee or agent engaged in the performance of investigative or prosecuting functions for an agency." This establishes the illegality of the relationship described in the question. Thus, answer A is incorrect. Moreover, neither disclosure (answer B) nor the ability to impose on the agency the burden of disproving inappropriate influence (answer C) is adequate to excuse this relationship as a matter of law.

72. Issue: APA Limits on Agency Heads' Supervision over Prosecutors

The correct answer is **A**. The bar on supervisorial relationships applies only to ALJs. Section 554(d) states "This subsection (554(d)) does not apply . . . to the agency or a member or members of the body comprising the agency." Thus, D is incorrect. Moreover, neither disclosure (answer B) nor the ability to impose on the agency the burden of disproving inappropriate influence (answer C) is necessary to establish the legality of this relationship, which exists in every agency.

73. Issue: APA Limits on Agency Heads' *Ex Parte* Contacts with Prosecutors

The correct answer is **A**. Section 557(d) restricts *ex parte* contacts with personnel *outside* the agency. Thus, B is incorrect. It prohibits such contacts. C is incorrect because Section 557(d) prohibits the making of any "ex parte communication relevant to the merits of the proceeding," which would include both clarifications and requests for more information. D is incorrect because the APA does not prohibit an ALJ from reopening a procedure.

74. Issue: Remedies for *Ex Parte* Contacts in Adjudication

The correct answer is **C**. Section 557(d)(1)(C) requires an ALJ receiving an external *ex parte* communication to disclose the substance of the communication on the public record. Thus, answer D is not correct. Answer A is not correct, as an immediate ruling against the communicating party is not required under the statute. Answer B is not correct, as the APA does not require a referral of the issue to the agency head to consider whether to rule against the communicating party.

75. Issue: Remedies for External *Ex Parte* Contacts in Adjudication

The correct answer is **C**. The first question is whether the association is subject to Section 557(d)(1). That section of the APA applies its restrictions to any "interested person." In a leading case, *PATCO v. Federal Labor Relations Authority*, 685 F.2d 547 (D.C. Cir. 1982), the D.C. Circuit interpreted this provision broadly, to include a labor union when the ALJ was considering whether another union had violated a federal law no-strike provision. Thus, presumably, a trade group would also be considered an "interested person" subject to the statute. Given this understanding, the same analysis from the previous question would apply: Section 557(d)(1)(C) requires an ALJ receiving an external *ex parte* communication to disclose the substance of the communication on the public record. Thus, answer D is not correct. Answer A is not correct, as an immediate ruling against Stepford (due to the communication of its allied party) is not required under the statute. Answer B is not correct, as the APA does not require a referral of the issue to the agency head to consider whether to rule against Stepford due to the communication of its allied party.

76. Issue: APA Limits on *Ex Parte* Contacts in Rulemaking

The correct answer is **D**. Section 554 applies only to adjudications; therefore, its restrictions on intra-agency *ex parte* contacts do not apply. However, Section 557 applies whenever an agency must act in accordance with Section 556 [see Section 557(a)]. In turn, Section 556 applies whenever an agency is required by Section 553 or 554 to act in accordance with its provisions [see Section 556(a)]. Section 553 deals with rulemaking; Section 553(c) states the conditions when an agency must act in accordance with Section 556. When one puts this analysis together, the result is that Section 557 applies to formal rule-making in addition to formal adjudication. Answer D reflects this combination [Section 554(d) not applying to rulemaking, but Section 557(d) applying].

77. Issue: "Arbitrary and Capricious" Review

The correct answer is **C**. The "arbitrary and capricious" standard is the default standard that a court applies when examining an informal agency action. See *Citizens to Preserve Overton Park v. Volpe*, 401 U.S. 402 (1971). Answer A is incorrect because the "substantial evidence" test is used only when an agency engages in formal action [see 5 U.S.C. Section 706(2)(E)], or when an agency's authorizing statute explicitly provides for a "substantial evidence" review. Answer B is incorrect because it states the test for due process review of a legislative action under the rational basis standard; this standard is too lenient for review of agency action. See *Motor Vehicle Mfrs Assn v. State Farm Mutual Auto. Ins. Co.*, 463 U.S. 29 (1983). Answer D is incorrect because the preponderance standard is not specified anywhere in 5 U.S.C. Section 706, the APA provision setting for standards of judicial review of agency action.

78. Issue: Reviewability of Agency Action

The correct answer items are I and II, which makes **B** the correct answer. I and II reflect the provisions in APA Section 701, that judicial review of agency action is available "except to the extent that (1) statutes preclude judicial review; or (2) agency action is committed to agency discretion by law." III is incorrect because statutes have been held to be drawn so broadly that they satisfy the "committed to agency discretion by law requirement" without violating the nondelegation doctrine. See, *e.g., Webster v. Doe*, 486 U.S. 592 (1988). IV is incorrect because it is generally understood that there is a presumption *in favor*, not *against*, judicial review. See, *e.g., Block v. Community Nutrition Institute*, 467 U.S. 340 (1984), recognizing the presumption in favor of judicial review even though in that case it holds the statute to preclude judicial review. This combination of correct answer items is reflected in answer choice B.

79. Issue: Statutory Preclusion of Judicial Review

The correct answer is **C**. This case is based on *DeMore v. Kim*, 538 U.S. 510 (2003), where the Court held that the statute at issue in this question did not preclude the alien's habeas claim. More importantly, C correctly states the presumption in favor of judicial review [see, *e.g., Block v. Community Nutrition Institute*, 467 U.S. 340 (1984)]. A is incorrect because it wrongly states that statutes precluding judicial review will be given a broad reading; this is wrong in light of the presumption in favor of judicial review. B is incorrect because it too is inconsistent with that presumption. See, *e.g., Bowen v. Mich. Academy of Family Physicians*, 467 U.S. 667 (1986), explaining the type of evidence that a court needs to decide that a statutory provision does in fact preclude judicial review of the claim before that court. D is incorrect because Congress can in fact draft statutes that preclude judicial review and has never said that such preclusion is more likely to be found only when "unimportant" rights are at stake.

80. Issue: Reviewability of Ongoing Agency Responsibilities

The correct answer is **A**, which correctly states the result in *Norton v. Southern Utah Wilderness Alliance*, 542 U.S. 55 (2004). In *Southern Utah*, the Court rejected a claim by environmentalist plaintiffs that an agency's failure to engage in proper management of wilderness areas constituted "agency action" reviewable by courts under the APA. Answer B is incorrect because the *Southern Utah* Court noted that the APA's definition of "agency action" includes failures to act. Answer C is incorrect because that definition does not expressly cover ongoing agency action, such as management of wilderness areas or national monuments. Finally, Answer D is incorrect because the APA does define "agency action," and that definition, as construed in *Southern Utah*, does not include failures to engage in ongoing action that a statute might require.

81. Issue: Reviewability of Agency Refusals to Initiate a Rulemaking

The correct answer is **C**, which states the result from *American Horse Protection Ass'n v. Lyng*, 812 F.2d 1 (D.C. Cir. 1987), an influential case on this topic. In *American Horse,* the Court held that the characteristics of a decision to decline to initiate a rulemaking (*i.e.,* the relative rarity of rulemakings and their primarily legal focus) distinguish them from refusals to prosecute, which are presumptively unreviewable under *Heckler v. Chaney*, 470 U.S. 821 (1985). Moreover, the fact that Section 553(e) of the APA authorizes persons to petition an agency to commence a rulemaking suggests that an agency's decision to decline that petition should be reviewable. However, the court also stated that such judicial review is extremely deferential. A is incorrect because such decisions are not presumptively unreviewable. B is incorrect because the "hard look" it suggests is inconsistent with *American*

Horse's statement that such review is deferential. D is a second-best answer, but its rule that a decision not to begin a rulemaking would be upheld so long as the agency provided a reason is probably too deferential even for the *American Horse* standard; at any rate, C is clearly a better answer, as it more accurately reflects that standard.

82. Issue: Freedom of Information

The correct answer is **B**, which correctly states FOIA exemption 5 [5 U.S.C. Section 552(b)(5)], which has been understood to preserve for the agency standard litigation privileges such as the work-product privilege. There is no "legitimate use" requirement for a FOIA request; thus, answer A is incorrect. Answer C is incorrect because there is no exemption for "information developed or created by the agency" (which, if it existed, would swallow much of FOIA's general disclosure requirement). Answer D is incorrect because there is no "other equitable reasons" exemption.

83. Issue: Freedom of Information

The correct answer is **B**. FOIA is a broad statute, and the request in this case probably doesn't fall under any of the exceptions to the information that FOIA requires be disclosed. See 5 U.S.C. Section 552(b), noting the exceptions. Answer A is wrong because while FOIA is a broad statute, it has more exceptions than the two mentioned in this answer [see Section 552(b)]. Answer C is wrong because FOIA does not impose this type of proof requirement on the party making the request. See Section 553(a)(3)(A), setting forth the basic rule that agencies must comply with valid requests. Answer D is incorrect, as there is no such limitation on FOIA.

84. Issue: "Reverse FOIA" Suits

The correct answer is **A**, which states the rule from *Chrysler Corp. v. Brown*, 441 U.S. 281 (1979). In *Chrysler*, the Court held that a party that has submitted information to the government may bring a "reverse FOIA" claim to seek to enjoin disclosure on the ground that disclosure would be arbitrary and capricious and/or violate another provision of law. B is incorrect because in *Chrysler*, the Supreme Court held that the exceptions are not mandatory; thus, this issue has been decided by the Court (and against the position CC would argue in this answer choice). C is incorrect because FOIA does not require that the requesting party prove that it has a legitimate interest in the information; thus, CC could not seek to enjoin disclosure on the ground that the group has not shown that interest. D is incorrect because *Chrysler* did approve of the general concept of a "reverse FOIA" suit under limited circumstances.

85. Issue: In-Camera Review of FOIA-Requested Documents

The correct answer is **D**, which reflects the text of FOIA. Section 552(a)(4)(B) provides that, if a FOIA request is not fully complied with, a plaintiff may sue to enforce compliance. Section 552(a)(4)(B) states that "In such a case, the court . . . may examine the contents of such agency records in camera to determine whether such records or any part thereof shall be withheld under any of the [statute's] exemptions. . . ." Thus, answer A is incorrect. This provision does not call for any approval of the review process by either party, and thus answers B and C are incorrect.

86. Issue: Burdens of Proof in FOIA Litigation

The correct answer is **D**, which reflects Section 552(a)(4)(B)'s text, which states, in relevant part, that "the burden is on the agency to sustain its action [denying disclosure]." Thus, answers A, B, and C are incorrect.

87. Issue: Reviewability of Statutory and Constitutional Claims

The correct answer is **B**, which states the rule and rationale from *Webster v. Doe*, 486 U.S. 592 (1988), the case on which this question is based. In *Doe*, the Court found the plaintiff's statutory claim unreviewable, but his constitutional claim reviewable, largely because of what it called the "serious constitutional question" that would arise if a colorable constitutional claim was held unreviewable. Answer A is incorrect because there is no doctrine of "pendant constitutional reviewability" that reflects the rule in that answer choice. Answer C is incorrect because there is nothing in *Doe* to suggest that the Court would strain harder to find a statutory claim reviewable as opposed to a constitutional claim, and the result and reasoning in *Doe* in fact suggest the opposite. Answer D is incorrect because the constitutional claim in *Doe* was not considered a political question. Answer B emerges as the best of these answer choices and is thus correct.

88. Issue: Exceptions to Notice-and-Comment Procedures

The correct answer is **A**, which states the general rule about when an agency regulation constitutes a "general statement of policy." See, *e.g.*, *Community Nutrition Institute v. Young*, 818 F.2d 943 (D.C. Cir. 1987). Answer B is incorrect because courts will review agency arguments that a particular regulation is simply a general policy statement; thus, agencies do not retain complete discretion (see, *e.g.*, *Community Nutrition*). Answer C is incorrect because such statements are exempt from the notice-and-comment process [see 5 U.S.C. §553(b)]. Answer D is incorrect because the exemption for these statements lies within the APA itself, not in judge-made law [see 5 U.S.C. §553(b)].

89. Issue: The Timing of Judicial Review

The correct answer is **C**, which correctly states the rule from *Abbott Labs v. Gardner*, 387 U.S. 136 (1967), which deals with the question of the ripeness of a challenge to agency action. Answer A is incorrect because *Abbott Labs* allowed the pre-enforcement suit to go forward in that case, finding no Article III problem. Answer B is incorrect because agency permission is not necessary for such a pre-enforcement challenge, and there is no such thing as "permissive jurisdiction" (at least in this context). Answer D is incorrect because Crow would have to satisfy the *Abbott Labs* test if it wanted to sue before being made the subject of an enforcement action.

90. Issue: Deference Levels for Agency Statutory Interpretations

The correct answer is **D**. The governing case, *United States v. Mead Corp.*, 533 U.S. 218 (2001), states that the vast majority of cases where the Supreme Court has granted *Chevron* deference to an agency's legal interpretation involve inter-pretations reached either through notice-and-comment rulemaking or formal adjudication. The Court also notes that this relative procedural formality is a good indicator of congressional intent to delegate to the agency the power to act with legal effect (*i.e.*, to act such that *Chevron* deference applies). Thus, procedural formality is doctrinally relevant to the correct answer, as well as predictive. Thus, neither item II nor item III is part of the correct answer. Item I is incorrect because *Mead* also makes clear that even an interpretation receiving no *Chevron* deference receives deference under *Skidmore v. Swift & Co.*, 323 U.S. 134 (1944). Moreover, *Mead* makes clear that it is at least possible that an interpretation not reached through notice-and-comment or formal adjudication procedures will still receive *Chevron* deference. See, *e.g.*, *Hospital Corp. of America v. Comm'r of Internal Revenue*, 348 F.3d 136 (6th Cir. 2003), giving *Chevron* deference to a regulation enacted without notice-and-comment procedures. Thus, no item is correct, which means the correct answer is D.

91. Issue: Deference Levels for Subsequent Agency Interpretive Decisions

The correct answer is **A**, which states the rule from *National Cable & Telecomm. Assn v. Brand X Internet Serv.*, 545 U.S. 967 (2005). In *Brand X*, the Court reasoned that giving *Chevron* deference in the second case was appropriate, even if it might mean upholding an interpretation that the court had rejected in the earlier case. The Court dismissed the argument that this approach allows the agency essentially to overrule the court because so long as the statute is ambiguous, the agency is not so much overruling the court as it is picking a different interpretation than the court's within a range of allowable alterna-tives. B is somewhat close, but it is ultimately incorrect because there is no special requirement that *Chevron* deference applies only in this situation if the statute is unusually ambiguous. C is incorrect because, as noted above, the *Brand X* Court rejected the "agency overruling" critique of its analysis. D is incorrect because *Brand X* makes clear that an agency doesn't lose its oppor-tunity to receive *Chevron* deference just because it earlier used a non-*Chevron*-eligible mode of reaching its interpretive decision.

92. Issue: Deference to Agency Interpretations of Its Own Regulations

The correct answer is **D**. This (somewhat complicated) situation was presented in *Gonzalez v. Oregon*, 546 U.S. 243 (2006), where the agency issued a regulation parroting the underlying statute, and then interpreted that regulation and claimed deference for that interpretation under *Bowles v. Seminole Rock*, 325 U.S. 410 (1945), and *Auer v. Robbins*, 519 U.S. 79 (1997). The Court in *Gonzalez* ruled that such parroting regulations do not merit *Seminole Rock/*

Auer deference. Answer A is incorrect because such deference does exist; it just wouldn't apply in this case. Answer B is incorrect because the agency would not receive this deference in this type of "parroting" case. Answer C is incorrect, again because *Seminole Rock* and *Auer* reflect a type of deference distinct, at least in theory, from deference under *Skidmore* and *Chevron*. Answer D reflects the existence of *Seminole Rock/Auer* deference, but also its inapplicability to this case. For this reason, it is the correct answer.

93. Issue: Deference Levels for Subsequent Agency Interpretive Decisions

The answer to this (again, complicated) situation is **B**, which states the rule from *National Cable & Telecomm. Assn v. Brand X Internet Serv.*, 545 U.S. 967 (2005), along the same lines as the answer to Question 91, above. In *Brand X*, the Court held that, in a case like this, the court has to examine its pre-*Chevron* opinion to determine whether it based its decision on a conclusion that the statute was clear. If it did, then the agency must lose again. However, if that earlier decision conceded the statute's lack of clarity but nevertheless reached its own decision without deferring to the agency, then the court would have to give *Chevron* deference to the new agency interpretation, assuming that it qualified for *Chevron* deference under *United States v. Mead Corp.*, 533 U.S. 218 (2001). Answer A is wrong because there is no such "last in time" doctrine in this context, and the *Brand X* Court explicitly rejected the charge that its analysis gave agencies the power to overrule prior decisions by appellate courts. Answer C is incorrect because as explained above, in some circumstances, the earlier court decision might not be given effect in light of the agency's new, *Chevron*-eligible, interpretation. Answer D is incorrect because it has the rule backward: only if the agency can prove to the court that the statute is *not* clear would deference be called for, which would, under *Brand X*, justify the court's reaching a decision different from the earlier one.

94. Issue: "Hard Look" Review

The correct answer is **A**, which correctly states the meaning of "hard look" review. See, *e.g.*, *Greater Boston Telev. Corp. v. FCC*, 444 F.3d 841 (D.C. Cir. 1970), coining the term "hard look" review by requiring that agencies have "taken a 'hard look' at the salient problems." There has been some confusion about this [see, *e.g.*, *National Lime Assn v. EPA*, 627 F.2d 416 (D.C. Cir. 1980), noting that "hard look" review has arguably come to mean that courts must take a hard look at agency action]; however, of the choices noted here, A is the best, and therefore it is correct. The other answers are incorrect, as they do not reflect, even arguably, the generally understood meaning of "hard look review."

95. Issue: "Substantial Evidence" Review

The correct answer is **B**. See 5 U.S.C. Section 706 (2)(E), requiring the court to "set aside agency action . . . found to be . . . unsupported by substantial evidence in a case subject to section 556 and 557 of [the APA — sections dealing with formal agency action] or otherwise reviewed on the record of an agency hearing provided by statute." Answer A is incorrect because informal agency action is reviewed under the "arbitrary and capricious" standard; see *Citizens to Preserve Overton Park v. Volpe*, 401 U.S. 402 (1971). Answer C is incorrect because standards of review don't vary based on judicial estimations of the importance of the issue at stake; rather, they are set forth in Section 706 of the APA. Answer D is incorrect because the APA's standards of review do not vary based on whether the action is taken by an independent agency. See, *e.g.*, *FCC v. Fox Television Stations*, 129 S.Ct. 1800 (2009).

96. Issue: Standards of Judicial Review

The correct answer is **C**, which is the best answer because it is explicitly supported by the APA. See 5 U.S.C. Section 706 (2)(E), requiring the court to "set aside agency action ... found to be ... unsupported by substantial evidence in a case subject to section 556 and 557 of [the APA — sections dealing with formal agency action] *or otherwise reviewed on the record* of an agency hearing provided by statute." (emphasis added). Compare *Citizens to Preserve Overton Park v. Volpe*, 401 U.S. 402 (1971); in arbitrary and capricious review, a court may uphold an agency action based on any information in the agency's possession. Thus, answer D is incorrect. Answers A and B are incorrect because despite some slight doubt on the issue, it is generally understood that the actual intensity of the judicial review of the agency's action does not turn on which review standard is used.

97. Issue: Identification of Due Process-Protected Interests

The correct answer is **C**, which correctly states the rule from *Sandin v. Conner*, 512 U.S. 472 (1995). Normally, a liberty interest of this sort would be determined by examining whether some state or federal law (*e.g.*, a statute, regulation, or even a prison manual) created an entitlement that gave rise in the recipient an objectively reasonable expectation that he or she would receive the benefit [*e.g.*, *Board of Regents v. Roth*, 408 U.S. 564 (1972)]. However, in *Sandin*, the Court recognized that bad effects flowed from converting trivial rights identified in documents such as prison manuals into due process–protected interests. For example, prisoners might have strong incentives to litigate due process claims, which might lead prison officials to remove such entitlements and vest more discretion in corrections officers. Thus, in *Sandin*, the Court required that, before sources such as prison manuals became the source of due process–protected interests, the interests at stake had to rise to some level of significance. For this reason, C is the right answer. A is incorrect because *Sandin* did not hold that prisoners give up all due process rights; indeed, its recognition that liberty interests had to be significant before they would be protected by due process suggests that prisoners continue to enjoy some procedural due process protections. B is incorrect because, as noted above, *Sandin* rejected complete reliance on *Roth*-type expectations analysis when determining whether the interest is protected by due process. D is incorrect because it also assumes complete acceptance of *Roth* in the prison context, with the caveat that the prisoner had to have been subjectively aware of the entitlement. As noted above, this is not the law after *Sandin*.

98. Issue: Agency Bias

The correct answer is **C**, which reflects the rule from *Tumey v. Ohio*, 273 U.S. 510 (1927), the case on which these facts are based. In *Tumey*, the Court held that such a scheme by its very nature violates due process of law, given the adjudicator's personal pecuniary interest in the outcome. See also *Withrow v. Larkin*, 421 U.S. 35 (1975), reaffirming and discussing *Tumey*. No particular proof showing needs to be made by the fined party; thus, answers A and B are incorrect. Answer D is incorrect because, as explained above, such situations do in fact violate due process, even short of a criminal conviction of the judge for corruption.

99. Issue: Deprivation of Due Process-Protected Interests

The correct answer is **D**, which states the rule from *Daniels v. Williams*, 474 U.S. 327 (1986). *Daniels* held that government action denying a person his or her property or liberty interest constituted a "deprivation" of that interest only if the action was intentional, rather than, say, negligent. Thus, answer A is incorrect. Answer B is incorrect because a malice requirement goes beyond what *Daniels* requires; government action may be intentional (and hence a deprivation) without it being motivated by malice. Answer C is incorrect because often there is a deprivation of an interest even though government gave advance warning of its action [*e.g.*, *Mathews v. Eldridge*, 424 U.S. 319 (1976); government still deprives an individual of a due process property interest in a disability check even when it warns the individual that it is cutting off the payments].

100. Issue: The Exhaustion Requirement

The correct answer is **C**, which accurately states the modern rule of exhaustion. See, *e.g.*, *McCarthy v. Madigan*, 503 U.S. 140 (1992), noting courts' "virtually unflagging obligation" to exercise jurisdiction given them, despite the exhaustion requirement, and setting forth three major exceptions to the exhaustion requirement. Thus, answers A and B are incorrect, as they suggest very limited, or no, exceptions to the requirement, which is in conflict with *McCarthy* and modern law more generally. Answer D is incorrect because the Court still acknowledges the exhaustion requirement as the general rule. See, *e.g. McCarthy* ("This Court has long acknowledged the general rule that parties exhaust prescribed administrative remedies before seeking relief from the federal courts."). Answer C correctly states the modern rule, which is balanced between these extremes.